AF615275

FISHING
WITH
SMALL FRY

by Jim Freeman

Chronicle Books, San Francisco

Printed in the United States of America

ISBN 0-87701-035-8

Library of Congress Catalog Card No. 73-77333

CONTENTS

Kids Natural Interest In Fishing	1
Purchasing Fishing Tackle	7
Casting	20
Plan A Trip	30
Lake Fishing	34
Stream Fishing	65
Expanding Your Fishing	80
Selecting Fly Fishing Equipment	82
Selecting Spin Casting Equipment	102
Selecting Bait Casting Equipment	105
There Is Something About Fishing	117
Index	120

KIDS NATURAL INTEREST IN FISHING

Back in Mark Twain's day, before kids even thought about "doing their own thing," they were actually freer. They could wander down a dirt road to the nearest fishing hole in an unpolluted creek or river with fishing poles over their shoulders and learn to fish by trial and error.

But most of today's Huck Finns, Tom Sawyers and Becky Thatchers grow up in cities or suburbs, far from dirt roads and unpolluted water. That doesn't mean, however, that youngsters today get any less pleasure and excitement out of fishing. In fact, getting 'back to nature' is an adventure and, coupled with youngsters real interest in ecology, fishing can develop into a life-long interest.

The first indication that you have a future fishing companion can spring up on a family vacation or camping trip. Or, it can be sparked by a friend's description of the battle with his first fish, which grows as big as Moby Dick in the telling. How can you encourage this desire to "go fishing?"

It can be a confusing and expensive desire to accommodate. If the sport were golf or bowling there are places available for experienced instruction. But, in most communities, there is no place where youngsters can learn fishing techniques. Schools require by law that youngsters learn one of the field sports which they will probably never use again after they reach maturity. This is unfortunate. In my opinion, outdoor recreation should be taught in the school system. So it's left to parents to develop children's natural interest by equipping and teaching them to fish.

In this book we'll start from scratch and assume a parent knows nothing whatever about fish and fishing. I believe even very experienced anglers could benefit from following the step-by-step instructions in this guide. I've seen many cases where experienced fathers have completely lost their chance to gain a lifelong fishing partner by expecting too much from the youngster on the first fishing excursion. Most anglers who are competent forget that a youngster is starting at the very bottom when he comes to the sport. It really bothers me to see a fishing father yelling at a youngster to "Loosen the drag, drop your tip, lift the bail!" when a youngster is fighting his first fish. The kid really doesn't know what he is being instructed to do, or why. Those first few trips are critical.

Every kid is an individual. Some learn very rapidly, others are slow at picking up new things. I think only the parents know the capacities of each of their children. Many non-fishing parents merely turn their kids over to a friend or relative when the subject of fishing comes up. This is wrong. By carefully pacing the learning sessions to suit the abilities of each youngster, something only the parent can know and do, a kid can learn fishing and have a lifelong hobby. The parent should be involved as much as possible in all stages of fishing. Fishing is, after all, one of the most enjoyable ways to have a good time, providing it is done correctly. Even a parent who never intends to become a fisherman should become involved at least to the extent of knowing what's going on. No parent should miss the absolute joy of the youngster's first good catch. Many times youngsters I've taught to fish have had the edge taken off their accomplishment and have lamented the fact that their parents missed the occasion.

All Kids Are Fishermen

Most parents assume only male children are interested in the sport of fishing. This is wrong. I've taught many kids to fish and have found that girls are just as interested and adept at fishing and fishing skills as boys. In fact, I've taught several girls I thought were a cut above most boys in learning the sport. This is probably a good place, therefore to explain that when I use "he" or "his" in this book I'm not slighting the girls, but only avoiding the cumbersome "he or she" or "his or her."

There is another item for the parent to take into consideration about teaching girls to fish that has social implication in the fishing world as it is developing today. The girl may well grow up to marry a fisherman. Approximately one American out of three will do some fishing during his life. If you go to popular fishing areas you will see every other boat has a man-and-wife fishing team. If the woman knows at least the rudiments of fishing, their fishing trips are a source of mutual enjoyment and her relationship to her husband very much eased.

In our modern society sports like fishing are increasingly becoming important sources of recreation and relaxation. When you look at our modern cities you see a concrete jungle. Kids who spend their entire life with nothing other than pavement and a few withered parks to look at cannot possibly know what a great place they have to live in and look forward to. Fishing and outdoor recreation in general can only broaden the base for understanding of the world, what makes it up, and what family participation in a completely wholesome sport can mean.

How Young To Start Kids Fishing

Many parents, particularly fishing parents, are concerned about the correct age to start a youngster fishing. The answer to this question depends very much on the specific child

A kid's first fish: a prize even if it won't make the record books.

A very small panfish can be a source of wonder to a very small fisherman.

Setting up equipment is part of the learning process.

involved. If you start youngsters at very much below the age of nine or ten you can't actually say you are teaching them very much. Kids under this age have an extremely brief interest span. I have met fishing fathers who had their kids doing some remarkably fine fishing even at these tender ages. In my own estimation even a five-year-old can get a lot of fun out of a fishing trip, even if he isn't paying enough attention to actually learn anything about the sport. At about six most kids can start handling a few of the easier-to-use fishing outfits. They will probably need a lot of continuous help, even after they've mastered the rudiments of casting, because their interest usually wanders during periods where fishing action is not fast.

PURCHASING FISHING TACKLE

It would be nice to say you can just go to your nearest tackle shop and at least get the basic equipment for successful fishing from a competent salesman. Unfortunately, this is the exception rather than the rule. I have talked with dozens of salespeople in tackle shops and found very few who knew very much about fishing and fishing equipment. I doubt many of these salespeople actually set out to cheat people in their purchases of equipment. I believe it's more a matter of ignorance. In any case, this book's first purpose is to guide the non-fishing family in making the first purchases. In the case of a widow or divorcee the situation can be even more critical, since a woman (more apt to be novice herself) can become easy prey for tackle salesmen.

Many newcomers to fishing are dismayed by all the equipment they see arrayed in tackle shops. They wonder just how complicated the sport of fishing is and whether they can both learn and teach the sport to their children. One of the nice things about fishing is that you can make it as complicated and demanding as you want or as simple as you want. To become a fisherman competent in all phases of the sport it takes at least the devotion you would assume is needed to make a winning professional golfer or tennis professional.

When the new fisherman sees the welter of equipment on display in tackle shops he or she immediately wonders if the sport is too expensive for the family budget. Again, like the subject of how complicated fishing can be, the sport can be as expensive or as cheap as you want to make it. Later in this book we will discuss specific equipment and equipment costs. Very probably it will cost more to transport a kid to the fishing area than it does to purchase the equipment. The transportation costs will depend on where the family lives in relation to the nearest water or to the nearest place where there is good fishing. I doubt any family budget is so tight the expense involved in fishing would be a very big burden. The main thing is not to spend your money on useless or nearly useless equipment.

Several Types of Outfits

There are several different types of fishing equipment. Each has its own use in one form or another in the fishing world. Some of this equipment is very specialized. In general, a newcomer to fishing should avoid any equipment that does not have a general use in many forms of fishing. No single type of equipment can be used for all different kinds of fishing; even though there are anglers with many years of experience who generally use only one type of equipment, such as fly fishing equipment.

When you are considering equipment to be used in teaching children to fish, you must also consider the ease with which each type may be used. Some kinds of equipment require very delicate handling. Others are so simple anyone can handle them.

Fixed Pole Equipment

Today you see very few fishermen using the venerable cane

When a youngster does most of the rigging and unhooking himself, the thrill of catching those first few fish is heightened.

pole for fishing. Yet for centuries cane pole or fixed pole fishing was developed to a fine art. I consider the simple cane or plastic pole to be the very best kind of equipment to use when you are teaching relatively young children to fish. Kids under six or seven years will rarely leave a bait alone long enough for a fish to take it when they are using equipment that has a reel. They seem fascinated by the operation of the reel and they want to continually reel the line in either to look at the bait or merely to be doing something. Even when they use a cane or plastic pole they will continually lift the bait from the water but they have a much better chance of getting a fish to hit because it takes far less time to lift the pole than to reel in a longer line.

Fixed pole fishing is the very simplest and cheapest form of equipment. A few dollars spent on a modern plastic pole, a length of line, leaders, hooks and sinkers are all that is needed. The line is tied to the slender end of the pole. Monofilament nylon of around ten-pound breaking strength is about right for fresh water fishing and fifteen-pound test is right for salt water fishing or fishing from a bridge, pier or dock. Some anglers prefer the ancient cane pole for this kind of fishing but I don't think this is a good choice. A cane pole generally comes as a one-piece affair of around nine or ten feet in length. This is much too long for transporting to the fishing spot and it must be tied to the roof of the car. The plastic pole can be disjointed so they can be carried in the trunk of the car.

There is little, if any, casting practice needed for fixed pole fishing. The line should be about half again as long as the pole. After tying the line on the tip of this rod store the additional line by winding it around the tip section between fishing trips and when moving to another spot to fish. Most fixed pole anglers use plastic bobbers. The bobber is placed on the line by means of a spring-loaded clip on the bobber. It is usually placed four to six feet above the hook, or hooks. A small amount of weight, usually just a couple of split shot (round pieces of lead that have a groove in them) is fastened to the line above the bait to keep it down in the water.

Baits For Bobber Fishing

Fishing with a bobber is naturally called bobber fishing. There are many different kinds of fishing bobbers but the common round ones are the most used. The size of the bobber used depends on which kind of bait you will be using. If the bait is to be worms, grubs or other small baits the smaller bobbers are best. If the type of fishing you will do requires using live baits like minnows, a larger bobber should be bought. The price of these bobbers is cheap enough so an angler should buy at least two or three different sizes for each fixed pole outfit.

It is best to wait until you get to the spot where you will do your fishing before you purchase baits. They may cost a few cents more than you could buy them nearer home but the local bait shops will have the proper bait for fishing in that area. The few cents you might save buying bait away from the fishing spot is hardly worth it for the first trip or two. In the case of live baits it's always best to buy near the fishing spot.

There are many different types of bait used in fixed pole fishing. Worms such as red worms, garden worms and nightcrawlers are popular in freshwater fishing. Red worms and garden worms (a smaller version of the nightcrawler) are best used for panfish such as bluegill, punkinseeds, perch and other small inshore fishes. Garden worms are more attractive to gamefish such as black bass or trout, probably because they are larger and more lively. Catfish can be taken on all kinds of worms but the bait must be fished right on the bottom. Live minnows, crawfish, crickets, grasshoppers, meal worms, dead minnows, prepared bait mixtures, even plain cheese, corn and breads can be utilized as bait. In choosing baits you can let your imagination go. However, be sure to get a free copy of the angling regulations in the state where you are fishing and check to see what kinds of baits are prohibited before you go fishing. Saltwater baits are numerous. Each area has specific baits preferred by anglers who fish that area. It is definitely a good idea to buy your saltwater baits at or near the spot where you will be fishing saltwater. There are so many different baits available and so many ways to rig them it would be impossible to describe all of them. However, most bait salesmen will tell you which bait to use, what kind of fish are available, how to rig the bait and where to fish them.

Even the youngest child can use and be successful fishing with the fixed pole outfit. The only drawback to using this kind of equipment is that you are forced to fish very close to the bank or boat. When you are fishing very close in it is usually necessary to keep movements to a minimum. A fish, in

Stone flies can be found under streamside rocks. A fishing trip can be an outdoor classroom in natural history.

clear water, is not afraid of the human shape providing it is not moving. Footsteps on the bank or on the bottom of a boat are felt as vibrations by fish in the water. I've found youngsters are much less likely to move around a great deal if you provide them with something to sit on. I include a camp chair as a basic part of my fixed-rod fishing equipment.

Most of the fresh and saltwater panfish and even some of the gamefish like black bass and striped bass are inshore species. At any sizable lake you will find nearly every cove or inlet well-endowed with bluegills and other sunfish. Most of the saltwater panfish are found lurking near the rocks along shore or under a pier or dock. This puts them well within range of a 10 or 12 foot fixed-pole outfit.

Buying Regular Equipment

Although the fixed-rod outfit can be a lot of fun to use and a productive way to fish for inshore fish, any fisherman—youngster or adult—will soon find need for equipment that allows more water coverage. There are four different types of equipment in general use by anglers. But before you go to the tackle shop to buy that first outfit you have to find out what kind of fish are readily available within reasonable distance of your home. All states have lakes and at least some streams that can be fished. If you live in the coastal states perhaps you will want to do mostly ocean fishing. In either case, now is the time to decide which kind of fishing you think you will be doing.

Revolving Spool Fishing

Revolving spool equipment is one of the oldest forms of fishing. It is also called baitcasting and level wind equipment by fishermen. I call it revolving spool fishing because this best describes the heart of this method of fishing. The spool on which the line is reeled has to revolve when a cast is made. Most anglers who use this method of fishing use a level wind reel (the reel has a guide that passes back and forth at the front of the reel so line is laid smoothly on the spool).

There are drawbacks to using this method of fishing when you are first learning to fish. First is the expense involved in this kind of equipment. The reel is a very delicate piece of equipment. Even though there are many cheap revolving spool reels on the market none of them are very good for fishing. Most reels worth owning will cost around $50 and up. The cheap "drugstore" outfits cannot be handled even by the most expert fisherman. When a cast is made you must put your thumb on the reel to stop the line from overrunning the spool and getting the line tangled just as the lure or bait hits the water. If you don't thumb the reel exactly right, the tangle you will get is called a backlash by anglers. Asking a youngster to learn this delicate method of fishing is too much.

Fly Fishing Equipment

Next to the fixed pole, fly fishing equipment is probably the oldest type of fishing still being practiced by anglers. It, too, is a delicate method of fishing. You can use fly fishing equipment for almost all fish but this is a very specialized way of taking fish. Everything must be perfectly matched in fly fishing equipment and the angler must be trained in the delicate timing just to make a cast. There are so many different elements that must be kept in mind by fly fishermen that this kind of equipment should be undertaken only after the youngster has learned how to fish.

Spin Casting and Spin Fishing Equipment

Spinning is so named because the line spins off the end of a fixed reel spool. There are two different types of spinning equipment, spin casting and spin fishing equipment. Either of these two methods of casting are good to use for teaching kids how to fish. The primary difference between the two methods is the way the reel is built. In spin casting equipment the face of the reel is enclosed by a shaped piece of metal; the line is run through a hole in this metal covering. This has the effect of stabilizing the line as it spins off the spool. With spin fishing equipment the reel spool is open, with no covering shield. The line spins directly off the spool and is stabilized by the large guides on the rod. There is some chaffing as the line is stablized by the increasingly smaller guides along the length of the rod to the tip but with proper weights this is hardly noticeable.

Although either type of spinning equipment is suitable for teaching youngsters to fish I prefer the open face spin fishing reels. The reason for this preference is that even with most careful handling of monofilament lines in any kind of spinning there is a certain amount of line twist and kinking. With the open face model reel the youngster, and his teacher, can spot a line snarl before it gets really serious. Often with spin casting reels, by the time you discover a snarled line, it is so tightly jammed under the cover of the reel it makes fishing hopeless. Let's simplify equipment selection and say you should choose a standard open-face model spinning reel.

Buying a Spinning Outfit

Good spin fishing equipment is not expensive. In fishing equipment, like equipment for any sport, you get what you

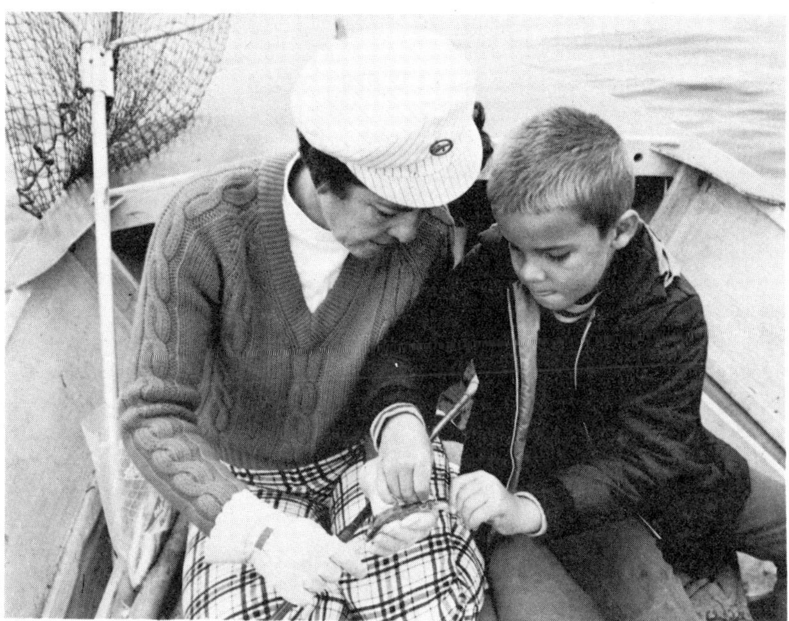

Rigging the gear is an important part of the sport of fishing and can bring the adult (teacher) and youngster (pupil) closer together.

pay for. But if the amount of money you have to spend is restricted, spend as much of the total as possible on the reel you purchase. In spinning the reel is the critical element. The rod used in this form of fishing can do a passable job even if it is very cheap. Of course, cheap rods will not have good fittings and the guides will wear out sooner than those on better-made models.

In the sport of fishing probably the cheapest thing is the cost of the equipment. This is true for the expert in all phases of fishing, or the occasional fisherman who fishes perhaps only during the annual vacation. It costs far more to pay for accommodations, boats, rentals, guides and merely to transport the family to the spot where the fishing is to be done. Good fishing equipment will last the average angler for a lifetime and it can even be handed down to future generations. It would be false economy to buy cheap equipment that will probably be difficult to use and perhaps ruin a trip because of some malfunction.

When you go to a tackle shop you will see many different models of spinning reels. The standard of the industry are reels like the Mitchell 300, the Diawa 7450 HRL and the Shakespear 2052 for fresh water fishing. These reels will hold sufficient line to fish almost all freshwater situations and many of the lighter saltwater situations. If you buy in a discount house none of these reels will cost much more than $20. If you watch the spring sales, just before the beginning of trout seasons, you may be able to buy the reels at a large savings over regular prices. If you are going to be doing most of your fishing in salt water the spinning reel to choose should be a bit larger, like the Mitchell 402 or the Diawa 7850 RL.

The first rod for fresh water fishing should be from 6½ to 7½ feet long and it should bend uniformly from tip to butt. This is what is called a progressive taper rod. All this means is that the taper, and the casting ability of the rod, is uniform throughout its length. When pricing and buying a rod pay more attention to the quality of the metal fittings than to the quality of the glass in the rod itself. I haven't seen a really poor glass rod for many years but I have seen very poor metal fittings on cheaper rods. There's a relatively new way of fitting the pieces of fiberglass rod together originated by the Fenwick Rod Company and now used by many other rod companies. Instead of using metal ferrules (the metal connection between the halves of the rod) the ferrules are merely the rod pieces formed in such a way that there is no ferrule at all, just the two halves of the rod. This is the type of rod I prefer and the type I suggest you buy. Most rod companies charge extra for this feature and it is worth paying the few extra dollars. With metal ferrules there is always a certain amount of binding when the rods are being used. On the rods without these metal connections there is never any binding or difficulty of getting the rod apart when you are through fishing.

The lines used in spin fishing are standardized today. Virtually all anglers use monofilament (plastic) lines. The price of monofilament can vary wildly from one brand to another.

The best combination to start with: A standard spinning outfit.

You can spend almost three dollars for 100 yards of name-brand lines. I suggest, instead of buying expensive lines during the learning process, buy the cheaper bulk lines. In large cities you can often buy a quarter pound of line for a dollar or two. This is a great deal of line in any of the smaller sizes. If you purchased a freshwater outfit with a seven-foot rod buy eight-pound test monofilament for your first quarter-pound spool. If you chose a light saltwater outfit with an eight or eight-and-a-half foot rod buy 12-pound test monofilament in a quarter-pound spool.

When teaching kids to fish the first problem you will have to solve is to teach them to cast reasonably well. Much of this training can be done on a front or back lawn or in a park. You will need some form of weight tied on the line to represent the weight of a lure or bait. If the tackle shop where you buy your equipment is fully supplied they will have practice weights on hand. These are generally rubber or plastic plugs shaped like a teardrop for good casting. They usually cost less than a dollar and are best to use for learning. However, if the tackle shop doesn't have a regular practice plug you can use lead weights. All tackle stores are well supplied with relatively cheap lead sinkers of all sizes. If you chose the freshwater outfit buy a few half ounce Dipsey sinkers to be used for casting weights. You should have more than one because when you are casting on grass or pavement there is a lot of line fraying caused by the friction of the line against these rough surfaces. The weights cost only a few cents each so buying a half dozen is in order.

It is important to good casting to load the monofilament line on the reel spool correctly. The first step is to set the rod and reel up with the spool empty and the bail open. String the monofilament through all the guides from the tip of the rod down to the reel. Tie the line onto the reel. Tighten the knot and push it down so it is snug against the reel spool. Pass a knitting needle, pencil or any other small object through the hole in the center of the quarter-pound spool of line. Have someone hold the spool and feather the edge as line passes from the spool to the reel. Hold the rod in the right hand and crank the reel handle with the left hand. Keep filling the spool until the level of the line is within about one-eighth of an inch of the curved lip of the spool. This is the proper level for line on a spinning reel spool. If this level is any higher line will spin off the reel in a clump and make a snarl of monofilament. If it is any less than this one-eighth inch measurement from the lip of the spool, casting will be difficult and the distances you can reach are lessened greatly because the line will rub against the lip of the spool.

When tying knots with monofilament you should always trim the end of the line in a Clinch Knot. A common fingernail clipper is ideal for this. Get into the habit of using a fingernail clipper right from the start or at least use a knife. Biting the line off with your teeth does work but you may break a tooth, as many anglers have, trying to bite off monofilament lines.

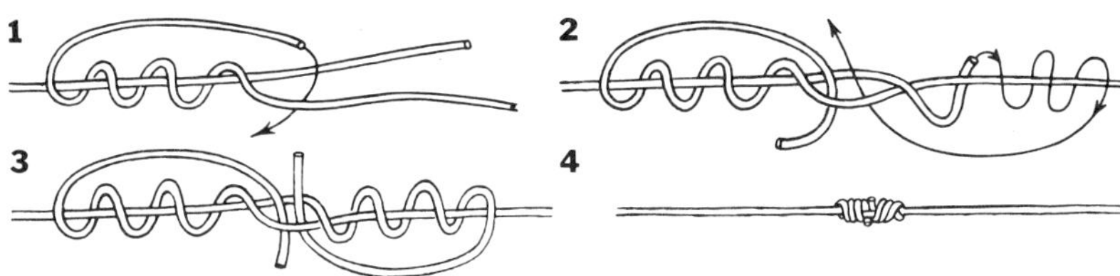

The Clinch knot is used to tie a monofilament line to a lure or fly. Thread line through eye of hook, or lure, wrap around the line several times (four or five times is ideal) and thread back through line opening in front of hook or lure. Pull tight while holding end of line. A double Clinch Knot is used to tie two lengths of monofilament together. It is called a Blood Knot when used for connecting two lines together.

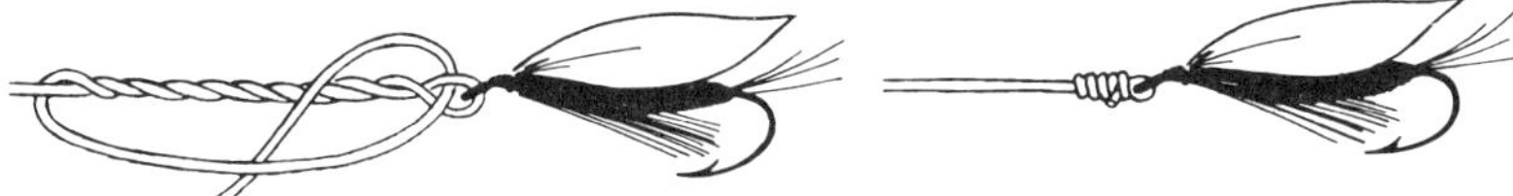

The Improved Clinch Knot is a stronger version of the simple Clinch Knot. This knot gives almost 100% knot strength to monofilament lines.

With the line extended a foot or two past the tip of the rod, tie on the half ounce Dipsey sinker or practice plug using the Clinch Knot.

When the weight or practice plug is reeled up to within about six or eight inches of the tip of the rod, casting practice can begin. At each stage of setting up the equipment, rigging the line and getting ready for the practice sessions the youngster should be included. In the case of very young children it is often best for the adult to do all of the knot-tying in practice and when actually fishing. For older youngsters there should be knot-tying sessions so they can tie their own knots when actually fishing. The youngster should be provided with a pair of fingernail clippers of his own so he is not tempted to bite lines off. The line used in knot-tying practice should be the same kind that will eventually be used for actual fishing. The adult doing the teaching should work at all phases of casting so he or she can pass on information to the youngster. But, as soon as it is feasible, the youngster should do all things necessary by himself. I'd suggest that you start by studying the pictures and captions.

CASTING

What's the proper method of casting with a spinning outfit? There are two techniques: Snap Casting and Lob Casting. The Snap Cast is the generally approved method for fishing with lures. However, many youngsters have trouble learning the timing required for successful Snap Casting. So, I suggest that you start with Lob Casting, which is fine for bait.

In Lob Casting—as you can see in the photos—the cast is made by hanging the line down a foot or more from the tip of the rod. This makes the arc described by the weight and the baited hook quite large, much greater than that in a Snap Cast. Although accuracy in casting is not as important in bait fishing as in lure fishing, the Lob Cast should be practiced for ease, familiarity and reasonable accuracy in advance of any actual fishing.

The proper position of the line is over the ball of the finger, not in the crease of the first joint and not pinched against the rod butt.

The start, or aiming position for the snap cast. Note how little drop is allowed between tip of rod and casting plug.

As the rod is snapped to the rear it loads up to supply energy needed for the cast. Here, the beginner does not put full bend into a snap cast.

The rod snaps forward and the plug is released. It takes practice to get the proper release point worked out.

The finger is pointed at the desired target on the forward snap.

Here is a fully loaded snap cast. With practice you can get maximum distance with a rod loaded this much.

After learning the basic casts it is often fun to experiment with special techniques like the "bow and arrow" cast. This is effective when fishing in areas with overhanging brush.

Casting Practice Can Be Fun

Casting practice sessions are, or should be, fun for both adults and youngsters. The first few casts, until the basic rudiments of casting are learned, should be made with no particular target in mind. A large enough space should be used so that no windows or other damagable objects are within range of even the longest random cast. Casting should always be away from any buildings instead of toward them. *There should also, naturally, be no people in the casting range.* With a half-ounce weight and eight-pound test monofilament line you can often cast as far as 200 feet, depending on wind direction. The ideal casting range is over water but a grass surface is just as good. Grass is less damaging to the surface of monofilament lines than concrete or other hard surfaces. Keep the practice sessions short, only as long as the youngster continues to show interest.

Casting Targets

Merely casting a weight into the distance can become boring once the rudiments are learned. The casts are correct when both the youngster and adult can cast the weight without lobbing it in a high arc. The arc of a good cast is relatively straight when Snap Casting. The Lob Cast arc is higher but the distances should be fairly close to those in the Snap Cast. As soon as you are confident that you and the youngster have the basics of casting learned it's a good idea to add some sort of target to the casting range. This target can be just about anything. A Hoola Hoop is perfect but you can also use a bucket, box or, even better, the lid off a garbage can. I prefer a metal garbage can lid because, when you manage to hit it, gives off a satisfying bong that takes away all doubt about whether you actually hit the target or not. If you have more than one target put them at different distances from the caster. In fishing you will have to continually change the distance of your casts and this is the best way to practice. Another way to vary the distance between casts is to move around.

The objective in casting practice is to duplicate as nearly as possible the situations you will meet once you get on a stream or lake. Once the casters are reasonably proficient in hitting targets in the open (one time out of five would be fairly good for beginners, although serious casters who compete in tournaments can hit a 30-inch target virtually 100 percent of the time) it's time to start making hitting the target more difficult. If you have a large yard with shrubs, the shrubs can be used to advantage. Merely place the target under a low-hanging tree or shrub. This means the caster has to concentrate or his weight will get hung up in the foliage. You don't have to have a tree. A clothesline, the stairs on the house (if they are open and clear of windows), or any other fairly high obstructions can be used to make things difficult for the caster. In actual fishing you will find many situations where the stream or lakeside cover is very difficult to cast under. Yet, if you wish to be successful, you have to manage to get a lure or bait very

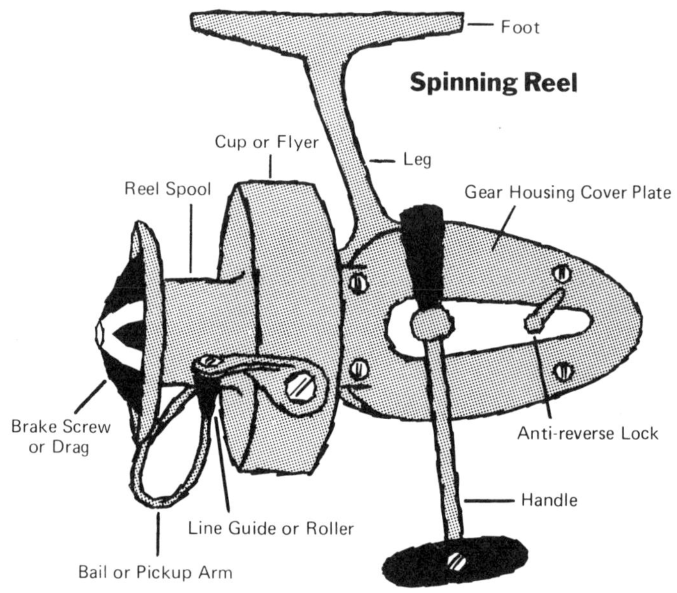

close, even in under the cover, before you can tempt a fish into hitting. The more variations you can include in the learning process, the more successful you are going to be in actual fishing, and the more interesting the lessons will become. It also gives both youngster and adult a lot of confidence when they are able to hit a partially hidden target a reasonable number of times during each casting session. Also, when you have a regular schedule of different methods of hitting the target it tends to extend the casting session for a longer period than if you merely cast at random.

Don't be surprised if the youngster learns how to hit that target better than you. Kids seem to learn this type of technique faster than adults. I've even found it a good idea to make a sort of game out of casting sessions, awarding recognition to youngsters (especially if they beat you). An hour or so each day for a week and both adults and youngsters will probably know more about casting a spinning outfit than most of the other anglers they'll meet when they actually fish.

A Hoola Hoop makes a great casting target. You don't need a swimming pool but if handy use one—it keeps line wear to a minimum.

A garbage can lid is another ideal target. It gives off a satisfying "bong" when you manage to hit it.

Once the beginner is proficient at hitting a target in the open, place it under some kind of obstruction. This gives practice in accuracy while adding fun to the practice session.

The next step is to simulate fishing from a boat. Place two chairs a few feet apart and continue casting. Here Kirk Savage is practicing a Lob Cast while his sister, Pamela is working on her Snap Cast.

If you think you might eventually do some fishing from a small boat it's also a good idea to include some casting practice in the sitting position. In a small boat it's dangerous for adults or youngsters to stand—your casting must be done from the seat of the boat. By providing a stool or chair, casting from the sitting position can be learned within a few short sessions. For a good safety drill set up two chairs about 10 feet apart for some of this practice, duplicating the area you'll be restricted to in a boat. You'll be surprised how much restriction there is when two anglers are this close together, particularly when the Lob Cast is being used. A great deal of care must be taken in a boat or the anglers may hook each other. You will find that when you want to make a Lob Cast to one side or the other you often have to drastically change your casting style, sometimes settling for a side-over lob to deliver the bait where you want to fish. It's much better to practice this at home where you can calmly discuss safety procedures for boat fishing.

Casting Clubs

Casting is a sport in its own right. There are many clubs set up whose purpose is holding tournaments and providing a group where the techniques of casting can be improved and enjoyed. If one of these clubs is within convenient distance of your home you should definitely think about paying them a visit. Usually if you ask around at local tackle stores or the local newspaper, you can get information about good clubs in the vicinity. It doesn't have to be a club established primarily for the purpose of casting. Most hunting and fishing clubs have casting clinics on a regular basis where they assist beginners in various phases of the sport of fishing. These sessions are mostly used to lure new members into the various clubs. You usually don't have to join the club in order to get the help the teaching members offer and the sessions are usually free.

PLAN A TRIP

Once the adult and youngster are familiar with casting techniques, and know how to tie the two basic knots illustrated in this book, it's time to think about planning a fishing trip. In fresh water the best times of the year to fish are usually early summer and early fall. During the winter, except in states with good fishing through the ice, weather and water conditions make fishing more difficult and the fish are not nearly as willing. During the hottest part of summer, usually July through August or September, the weather and water are too warm in most areas for good fishing. In ocean fishing the summer months are usually the best time for most inshore fish. At this time of year saltwater fish are feeding heavily, preparing for the less food rich winter months. You don't have to postpone a trip if you have become proficient at some other time of year but you should realize that your task of tempting fish is much better at the right stages of the seasons.

Information From Newspapers

Your local daily newspaper probably has a column on fishing and the outdoors. Smaller newspapers usually do not have very complete coverage of this subject but virtually every larger metropolitan newspaper covers fishing on the sports page. Most outdoor columnists detail where the best fishing is and what kind of fish are being caught. This is important information when planning the first few trips with a youngster. Conditions change drastically as the seasons progress. An area, lake or stream that is giving up good strings of fish one week may be very poor to fish the very next week. This is what the outdoor columnist is paid to tell readers. A good outdoor columnist will not only tell his readers what kind of fish are being taken but what they are being taken on. If baits are most effective he will say so. If lures of a certain type are best this information will be in the column. The important thing is that the information in these columns is up-to-date and detail the changes in fishing conditions as they occur.

Fish and Game Departments

Every State (and Provinces in Canada) has a Fish and Game Department. This department might be called a game department or resources department but, whatever the name, you can be sure each has a regularly staffed agency to see to the welfare of fish and game. You should get copies of the department regulations and study them with the youngster. Most of these agencies publish guidance material in some form that will tell fisherman the location of places to fish and what there is to be caught. Some states do a good job of providing this information. Others are lax on the subject. But any information concerning what there is to fish for is important to a beginner. Usually the main office of the Fish and Game Department is located in the state capital. You should make an effort to find this agency in your state, or in a state you wish to fish and write them a letter stating that you are new to fishing and would like any booklets or information they can send you to acquaint yourself with fishing in that state. Usually this information is free, sometimes there is a small cost for printed material. Study the information you receive carefully. Often it is so complete, including times of year to fish and how to catch the fish available, that most of the problems of deciding where and when to fish are solved merely by reading the material. In any case you will have a way of knowing what fish are available.

Guides

For the father or teacher of a youngster it is very worthwhile to consider the merits of hiring a guide for the first few days of fishing. Most areas where there is good fishing will have guides available for hire, just as you find partyboats in saltwater areas. On the surface it might seem like a large expenditure of money to hire a guide, who probably has to charge from $30 to $50 a day to pay for his time and amortize the costs of equipment such as boats and specialized fishing gear needed to take fish in his particular area. If you consider the situation, however, you may agree that hiring a guide for those all important first few trips makes a great deal of sense.

First of all, you have already invested money in equipment, as well as time in learning how to use it. You will spend at least some money getting to the area where you are going to fish, and you may also have to spend money for accommodations and boat rental. The few extra dollars spent to hire a competent guide may well be the best possible investment to make at this point. Successful guides, those who have been in the business for any length of time, are men who consistently produce fish for their customers. If they didn't they would soon be out of business because in the angling fraternity fishermen pass this type of information around among themselves.

There's a second consideration when it comes to hiring a guide, one which is not often taken into account by most anglers. You are actually buying years of experience in fishing a given spot. During the day with a good guide you can quiz him about what you are doing and why you are doing it. In the course of this conversation you and your youngster can gain more knowledge than you could in many, many trips to that specific body of water. In fact, I know many guides who hire another "pro" in an area new to them in order to find out the tricks of fishing the new area in a very short time. I also know many adept fishermen who know a great deal about fishing who always make it a point to hire a guide for the first few days of fishing a new area, even though they own and know how to use all the necessary equipment for fishing in virtually any situation. I do this myself when I am going into an area for the first time, although I own more equipment than most any fisherman and use it to make a living.

Importance of the First Trip

The first few fishing trips are critical when you are dealing with youngsters. In some cases they make the difference between continuing interest or indifference. Do everything possible to assure success during the first few trips. If youngsters have to fish hour after hour, even day after day, without catching any fish it is very easy for them to lose all interest in the sport. But if the youngster is successful right from the start the chance of continued interest is much greater. An adult may become interested in fishing as a way of relaxing and simply enjoy the opportunity to get away from normal routine. But a youngster wants to catch fish. In picking the spot and type of fish to try for you also have to consider the tastes of the vast majority of youngsters. Where an adult would consider a beautiful trout a worthy fish a youngster usually doesn't care what he catches as long as he gets action.

LAKE FISHING

In fishing most lakes it's usually a good idea to seek out areas that have streams feeding into the lake. These are natural gathering places for fish of all kinds because the incoming flow of water generally provides an abundance of food that rides along on the currents of the inflow. The area near an inflowing creek is also apt to provide a variation of temperature in the lake water that certain species of fish prefer. A good map of the lake you intend to fish will be a big help in locating these premium spots near inflowing creeks and rivers. If one isn't available, simply ask the people at the marina or tackle shop near the lake where these spots are. (In salt water the same thing applies, except that the flows are generally caused by tidal movement or by currents in the main body of the ocean or bay. You have to get local advice when seeking these spots.)

It pays to be alert in any kind of fishing but it is a particularly important element in lake fishing. Each lake will have its own pattern of activity as it concerns the fish population. Almost every time you fish a lake you can learn something new about it. This is one reason I suggest you pick a single lake, or just a few of them, and return as often as possible. The pattern of fish activity in a single lake will change not only with the hours of each day but also with the seasons. You might find a single point of land jutting out into the lake that always produces fish in the evenings or mornings, though it may be barren of fish at any other time as far as catching them is concerned. Again you may find certain coves swarming with panfish at certain times of the year and certain times of day. This is the sort of information that will become invaluable to you for consistent success.

Fresh Water Panfishing

Fishermen use the term panfish to denote any freshwater (and sometimes saltwater) fish that is too small to be considered a gamefish. This includes fish such as bluegill, crappie (pronounced croppy) bullheads, sunfish (like punkinseed, redbreast, red-ear), rock bass and perch. In the context used here I would also like to include smaller black bass (largemouth and smallmouth), planted trout, catfish of all kinds, and any other available inshore fish your area may support.

To most kids, especially the younger ones, a four or five inch bluegill is just as much fish as a fighting rainbow trout. Panfish like bluegill and perch are normally much easier to take and much more readily available. This is not always the case, and I will detail the exceptions, but generally panfish are the best kind of fish to start on.

After checking with the game department and other sources, such as the daily paper and local sportsman groups, the adult who wants to get the youngster into fishing action on the very first trip will probably come to the same conclusion I have—that the best bet is freshwater panfishing.

I have found that small black bass and planted rainbow trout, or other species of freshly planted trout, are relatively easy for kids and newcomers to angling of all ages to take. In fact, if your state has a regular trout planting program it is often possible to discover, from published information, just where fresh plants of trout or other fish are to be made.

I am not suggesting that you train a youngster in how to track down a hatchery truck to find good fishing. Most anglers everywhere frown on this sort of thing. But if you can't find any other convenient outlet for fishing the hatchery planting schedule is useful at least for the first trip or two with a youngster. As soon as you have managed to whet the appetite of the youngster for the game of fishing following the hatchery truck should be discontinued. These fish are meant to be caught and if you only take a limit it is within the law to fish this way.

You should try to determine exactly which kind of panfish are available. This may seem easy but it isn't in some cases. First of all, fish may go under a number of different aliases, depending on locality. Often a bluegill, for instance, can be called by local names such as bream, sun perch, blue sunfish and copperbelly as well as the accepted name of bluegill. The red-ear goes under other local names such as shellcracker (so named because they have grinding bones in their throat to break up crustaceans) stumpknocker and yellow bream. The redbreast sunfish can be called yellowbelly sunfish, longear sunfish, sun perch or redbreast bream. I'm certain there are other local names for the different species of panfish but make an effort to find out just which one you are going to be fishing for.

The bluegill looks a great deal like many other members of the sunfish family, such as the red-ear and redbreast, but there is a big difference in how the species react to baits and lures. The bluegill and redbreast sunfish will readily take most small baits, as well as small under-surface and surface lures. (This is particularly true of the redbreast.) The red-ear sunfish, however, spread out a great deal more than bluegill and it is difficult to locate enough of them in one place to make up a fair-sized stringer of fish, except at spawning time in early spring when they go on the beds in shallow water. As noted above certain panfish are difficullt to take while others, like the redbreast sunfish readily take most angler offerings. The pumpkinseed of the northeastern United States (not called anything else, unless it would be common sunfish), which has been planted all over the country, is as willing or even more willing to hit than the bluegill or redbreast.

When it comes to black bass, only two types are now widely distributed in most of the nation's water: the largemouth and the smallmouth bass. Another species, the redeye bass, is becoming more widely distributed but, in its action and reactions to angler's offerings, this type of bass is so similar to the smallmouth that little differentiation need be made between them. In fact, it is even difficult to tell the two species apart when they are side by side on a stringer.

I consider fish like the black and white crappie, yellow and white bass species the least desirable to seek on the first few fishing trips unless you have no other alternative. These fish are schooling species and locating schools in a large lake can consume a great deal of time. This kind of fishing is very dull for youngsters. However, is you have local advice on exactly where to find these species by all means fish for them. Usually when you do locate schools of any of these fish the action for the fishermen is fast and furious, just what you want to add excitement to a youngster's first few days of fishing. If you find special circumstances, as where crappie are gathered under docks and under lights at night, by all means make use of this information. It's a lot of fun for every member of the family.

In general bottomfishing for fish like catfish, bullheads or even carp should be avoided for the first few trips. Again, the exceptions are when you have some special knowledge about where concentrations of them may be found or when you have no alternative. These species are willing enough and worthy of an angling effort but it may take a long time to locatc concentrations of them where you can get exciting fishing.

Panfish Technique

As a general rule fish like bluegill, perch and rock bass are not fished for enough to keep their populations in any body of water under control. These species thrive in large and small lakes, slow flowing streams and even in millions of farm ponds throughout the country. When they are under-harvested they tend to become stunted. This is caused because there are so many fish competing for a limited supply of food. But kids seldom care about the size of the fish they are taking. A stunted panfish is just as much fish to them as the game species.

Sunfish of all types are usually not hook or line shy. Rigging for sunfish and other panfish fishing is relatively simple. The most-used terminal rig consists of a small bobber placed from three to five feet up the line from the bait. The best hook to use is a No. 10 or No. 12 long shank hook. The reason for the long shank is that it is easily twisted to remove it from a fish's mouth. A pair of split shot can be clamped on the line a foot or so above the baited hook to keep the hook and bait down in the water.

I generally rig my own sunfish terminal rig in a different manner than other anglers. If I only have a reel fitted with eight or ten pound test line, I wind on about 50 to 100 feet of four pound test line right over the top of the heavier line. I've found that the smaller line is much better for handling the very light floats and weights that are best for bait fishing for sunfish. You don't have to fill an entire spinning spool with small line because panfish will not take any extra line off the spool once they are hooked. Generally short casts are all that are required to reach the best spots for sunfish.

The choice of suitable baits is wide and varies from one part of the country to another. Garden worms, manure worms, crickets, roaches and grasshoppers (live or dead) all have their part in panfishing. If I am going to baitfish for sunfish I personally prefer common garden worms. I specify garden worms to seperate them from nightcrawlers. The larger night-crawlers are seldom suitable for taking sunfish because they are physically too large for these smaller fish. In most parts of the country other worms such as red worms are sold in bait-shops. The same goes for nightcrawlers. You can seldom find garden worms of the proper size for sale. If you have a front or back yard, it is simple to get a supply of garden worms. Just keep one section of a garden plot wet for several days and garden worms will gather. It can be fun for kids to dig up their own worms before they start on a trip. Worms can be kept alive for quite a length of time in a can or bottle that is about half filled with a mixture of dirt and grass cuttings. They should be kept as cool as possible and airholes should be punched in the bait container lid.

Some parts of the country have special types of baits for sunfish such as catalpa worms, bonnet worms, meal worms or golden grubs. Any bait shop will sell the proper baits for fish in that area. Any live or prepared bait is suitable for sunfish fishing and it's generally a good idea to use the most popular bait in each area. You can be sure anglers in each area have tested all forms of bait and have found that one that is best for taking local fish.

Lures For Panfish

You need not confine your fishing for sunfish and other panfish to baitfishing. Most of the panfish of all types will readily take many different types of artificial lures. In fact, for the first few trips I suggest you use a combination of bait and lure instead of limiting yourself to just using baits. During some times of the year sunfish and other panfish actually prefer lures to any form of bait. A very effective combination for bluegill and other inshore panfish can be made by using a worm-baited hook on the end of the line and a fly on a dropper strand (a short length of line tied to the main line) a foot or so above the end of the line. A split shot can be clipped to the line for additional weight. Almost any kind of small fly is effective for taking most panfish species. Flies in sizes No. 8 through No. 12 are a good choice. The name of the fly is unimportant but I prefer flies with a generally drab appearance such as the Black Gnat, Gray Hackle or any of the imitations of underwater insects (called nymphs). The dropper strand that attaches the fly to the main fishing line should be about a foot long. If you want to cover all possibilities you can also add another lure to the line just below the spot where the bobber is attached to the line. I prefer a high-floating lure like a rubber

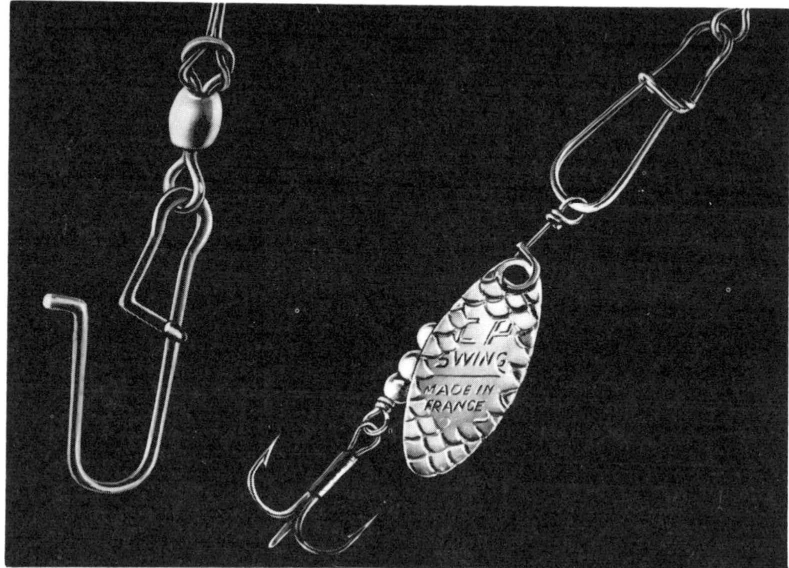

This type of snap swivel attaches and locks twice: first to the end of the line and then to the lure.

spider for this lure at the surface. Tie another dropper strand to this lure about a foot long. The spider will float out some distance from the bobber. It can be very exciting for young and old to watch this surface lure until a sunfish surfaces to hit it. This type of lure is also effective for taking some other species like black bass. It can be the high point of any trip if black bass or panfish surface to hit a lure where you can actually see the action as it happens.

If you and your youngster decide to fish with lures in preference to baitfishing you have to rig a bit differently. For fly or spider fishing you should tie the float or bobber to the end of the line and tie the fly, or flies, to the line a short distance up the line from the bobber. This is a particularly effective way to take fish like bluegill and punpkinseed. In any lure fishing for any panfish species the lure or fly should always be moved very slowly. You needn't fish near or on the surface.

One of the most effective rigs for lakes that have gamefish as well as panfish is made by replacing the bobber on the end of the line with a floating, diving or sinking lure and still tying on one or two flies a foot up the line from the lure. With this combination you are offering the lure to the game species and the fly or flies to the panfish. When moved slowly through the water a rig that combines a lure on the end of the line with a fly a short distance up the line resembles a small fish chasing an insect. It is surprising how often you manage to take more than one fish in a single cast. Imagine how exciting this would be to a kid! Evidently when a panfish hits the fly and begins towing it around gamefish like bass and trout get excited. They will hit the larger lure during the battle to subdue the smaller fiish. For this type of rig I generally prefer to use the heavier eight or ten pound test line on the main spool, rather then the lighter four pound test. Often gamefish taken with this rig can be very respectable in size. They are also capable of tangling the line on the bottom so the extra-strength line comes in handy.

Fish Slowly

I would like to stress here that it is impossible to fish a lure or bait too slowly to suit any of the sunfish or most of the other panfish. A bluegill or pumpkinseed will fin up close to a surface lure that is laying still in the water. Often they even back off and eye the lure from different angles before they approach it again. Fast movements of any kind frighten panfish. Bluegill will often approach a popper being fished for black bass and quickly swim off as the slightest popping noise comes from the plug. Just as often, when a school of panfish are actively feeding, the bait or lure will be hit by an eager fish. But even when they are feeding avidly they will shy away from a fast moving lure.

I have found that many youngsters aren't willing to leave a lure or bait in the water very long before they want to reel it in and inspect it. Don't shout at a youngster who does this. Instead, try to direct attention to something else while the bait or lure has a chance to sink down to the level where it can attract fish. In extreme cases use two rods, one for the youngster to reel in and one for actually catching fish. I've found kids generally do not care whether they hook fish or someone else does, as long as they are handed the rod to reel in the fish. This is a device most adults would object to but it's about the only solution for a youngster who does not move the lure or bait slowly enough or leave it in the water long enough for a fish to hit.

Schooling Panfish

I mentioned before that the first few trips you should not try for schooling panfish like white or black crappie, rock bass or yellow or white perch. If sunfish are available, however, these species can be fun to fish for and they often appear inshore where you can get at them without having to rent or buy a boat. At certain times of the year, such as spring and again in the fall, schooling panfish will move in certain ways. Local anglers know this and they form a tradition of being in the right spot at the right time. Often you can get special information about "runs" of fish like crappie, perch and rock bass from local anglers (or the outdoor writer on a newspaper). If so, make plans to join the local anglers for the big annual fishout for your first trip. These items are a matter of local research and they vary so much from one location to the next you simply have to make local inquiry.

If you have no special information and cannot locate sunfish to try for on the first few trips you can still try for these schooling species. Each has its own set of preferences. If you've determined a body of water (almost always a lake) has crappie in it, search out shoreline areas that have some sort of brush or vegetation cover. Both white and black species of crappie have a distinct craving for areas that have brush. They feed extensively on smaller fish and these smaller fish generally find cover and protection from predator fish in brush or weeds. Often you can shorten the job of locating brush in a larger lake by simply asking someone at lakeside, like the tackle dealer at a marina, where crappie are usually taken in that section of the lake. If you cannot get specific information begin to move along the shore of the lake and cast with a wobbling spoon, a small colorful leadhead jig (a lead lure with shaped head and embedded hook) or a lightly hooked live (or dead) minnow of small size on the line. The thing to avoid is staying in one place if you are not hooking crappie. Use your watch. If you haven't gotten a bite within five minutes, and you haven't seen another angler catch a crappie, move to another spot along the lake shore. Repeat this process of moving and casting until you do start getting hits. Crappie are avid feeders and they will hit readily if they are in the area being fished.

Rock bass are much the same. They are found in rocky areas along the East Coast where they feed in brackish (partly salty) water. They are just as avid in their feeding habits as the crappie. For white bass you usually need a boat. These fish are not normally found in inshore areas. They school at median depths out in the open waters of the lake.

Perch are also much like crappie. They can be found near shore and around and near docks and piers. You have the same problem of locating a concentration of them so keep moving until you begin taking fish. Perch hit nearly any bait anglers offer them.

There will be certain preferences in each new body of water and you should try to learn what experienced anglers use to take their fish. You can probably get local advice on where your best chances are in each new lake if you tell the angler you are teaching your youngster to fish and need help. As a matter of common sense if you see another angler hauling in fish after fish (as is the case when there is a big school of panfish) and you are not taking them, walk up or row over to him and ask his secret. I've never seen a case where a successful angler wasn't willing to share his knowledge with a beginner. Usually you can hardly shut him up once you acknowledge him as an expert and ask him for advice. Some anglers are very protective when it comes to information on special fish like trout. This is not the case when you are asking about panfishing information.

Gamefish

Gamefish like black bass and trout should not be ignored for the first few trips, especially if you have some special know-

Leadhead jigs and worm combinations come in a wide variety of colors and sizes.

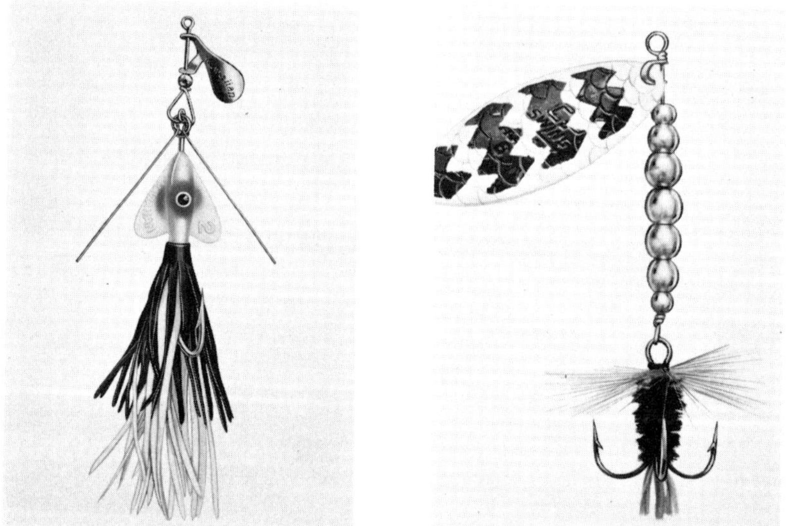

This is the ideal type of lure to use where there is a lot of brush and rocks since it is virtually weedless and snagless.

A standard spinner that will take nearly any game or panfish species. This type of lure needs no additional weight to cast.

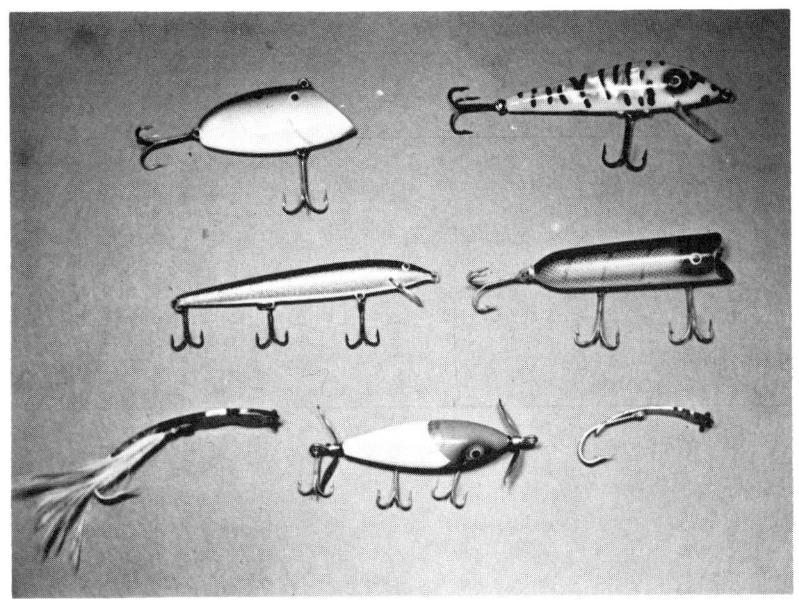

A variety of lures that can be used to take gamefish like black bass and striped bass.

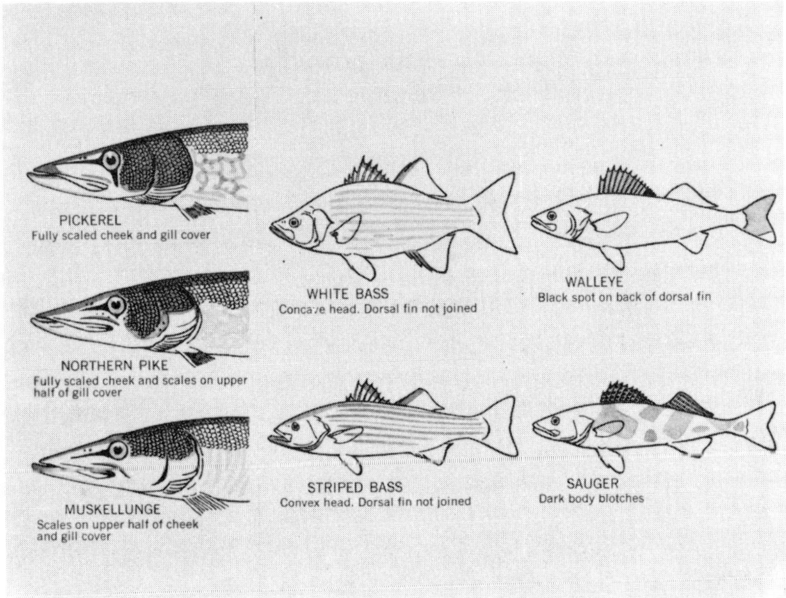

"What kind of fish is that, Daddy?" Here's a quick guide to help you identify some of the popular gamefish.

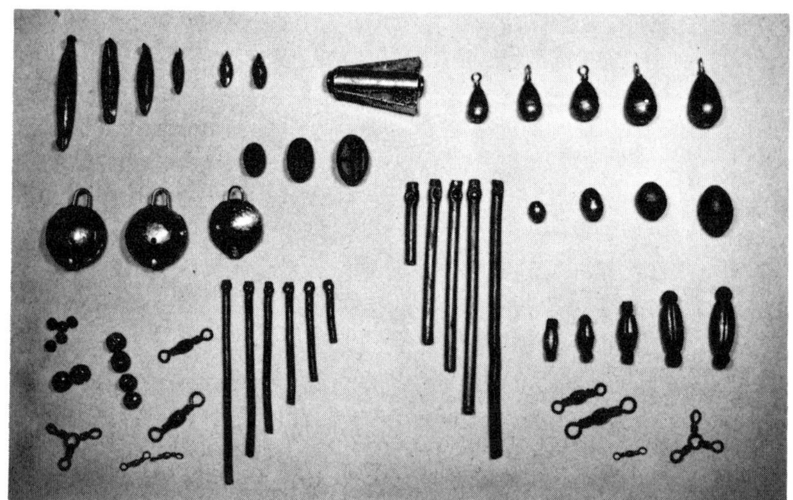

These are some of the different types of weights used in fishing, and the swivels (bottom, left and right) used to keep the line from twisting. The long leads in the middle are "pencil sinkers," used where there are a lot of snags in the water.

ledge that fishing is good for these species at a given spot. Often you can find excellent prospects for these glamor species at specific spots by reading the newspaper column on fishing. At special times black bass, trout, saltwater species like striped bass or bluefish, and many others, are as easy to catch as the panfish species. And just because they are large and glamorous doesn't mean you should shy away from them simply because you are a beginner. In fact, the conditions of water temperature and muddiness will always control the actions and reactions of fish to baits and lures. The main reason larger individual specimens of gamefish are more difficult to take is not because they are any smarter than the smaller individuals. Rather, when gamefish get larger they develop different habits from the smaller fish in each species. Larger fish usually only come into the shallower area near shore very early and late during the day. The rest of the day they stay in deeper water. This means they are harder for shore fishermen to reach and is the reason so few of them are taken by shorebound anglers. Smaller individual gamefish are much more likely to be in shallower water near shore because they find the food they need in areas where light reaches the bottom to generate food growth. They also find the protection and cover they need to avoid becoming a meal for larger fish.

In coastal areas you will find fishing is very much affected by migrations of almost all saltwater fish. These are the famous runs you can read about in the daily newspapers. Each area along the coastline will have a set pattern of runs of different species. You can usually find out where the runs occur by asking at tackle shops and sportsmen clubs. Normally the runs are on when fish move in close to shore where a lot of anglers can get at them at the same time. Just as often you will find that a boat is essential for taking fish from these runs. In most saltwater areas there are boats for hire (usually called partyboats) where, for a set amount of money, you can hire the boat (along with a number of other fishermen) for a day of fishing. In many cases this is the way to get action, especially on those first few trips when you are trying to find action for a youngster to keep up his interest.

Black Bass Fishing

If you decide to try for black bass there are certain things you should know about the species. The most important thing is to realize that black bass of all species are bottom-dwelling fish. This may seem basic but most anglers seem to ignore this simple fact when fishing for bass. They waste most of their time fishing for bass in areas that seldom, if ever, contain any bass to be hooked. You may know that black bass are famous among anglers for hitting surface lures at certain times of the year and certain times of the day. But, when they are hitting surface lures they are in comparatively shallow water right up next to shore. Normally, about 90 percent of the bass hooked are hooked on lures that either dive or sink down to near the bottom.

In lake fishing for bass one of the best investments you can make is to either buy or rent a boat and outboard motor. Just as hiring a guide makes sense, the $10 or so spent to rent a boat and motor is a good investment, especially for those all important first few trips. The boat provides the mobility you need to fish a great amount of water in a single day. In shore fishing you can only fish a nominal amount of shoreline in a given day. With the motor and boat you can fish many miles of shoreline in a single day, any of which could contain the only willing fish in the lake. You can learn to operate an outboard motor in a matter of a few minutes instruction by the rental agent.

If you decide to fish for black bass from shore the same rule about moving around applies as for panfish or any other species. Don't stay in one spot for very long. If you don't get a hit within about five minutes move to another spot. Unlike most panfish species which school up in large numbers, black bass generally do not school, so even if you do get a fish in a certain spot it is generally better to continue to move along the length of the shore rather than to stay in that spot. Even if you can see other black bass in a cove or off a point it is very doubtful you will be able to hook more than a few of them in any one spot, unless it is a very special situation. Black bass of all sizes are noted among anglers as being the smartest of all the freshwater fish. They soon learn to avoid the same offering that has taken a few fish from any one area. The exception might be when you are fishing over a group of smaller bass, but this situation is so rare it is hardly worth counting on. If you see a number of bass in a given spot and want to keep fishing there, at least change the method or lure you are using after you hook a few of them. This is about the only way you can load a stringer with bass. The exception might be during the spring when bass go on the spawning beds and where many of them are spawning in a single area. When bass are on the spawning beds they will attack anything that moves near the nests.

Bass Fishing With Minnows

One of the simplest ways to take black bass is with live or dead minnows. I prefer the largest minnows I can find for bass fishing. With large minnows it's usually not necessary to use

Literally hundreds of sizes, shapes and colors of plastic lures are available. Here is a variety of lures that will be taken by nearly all fish.

any weight to make them heavy enough for casting. However, I generally add a couple of large split shot to the line a few feet up the line from the minnow to force the minnow to swim down to the bottom. A lively large minnow can be very stubborn about staying near the surface, knowing very well that if he gets into deeper water a predator fish may very well catch him. The split shot will take him down so the predator bass can do just that. You can also fish a minnow with a bobber by rigging it the same way you rigged for panfishing. (The same thing goes for larger nightcrawler worms.)

However, the single hook through the lips, nose or just under the flesh at the top and back of a minnow is the very best way to fish for black bass. The main thing is to not fish the minnow in one spot for any long period of time. If you are fishing from a boat, move slowly along shore and cast the minnow in toward the bank, just as you would if you were using a lure. This is one of the most efficient ways of luring black bass, especially the larger individuals. Few other anglers I've ever met fish minnows this way. Most prefer to stick with the bobber, even though it is apparent, if you'll stop to

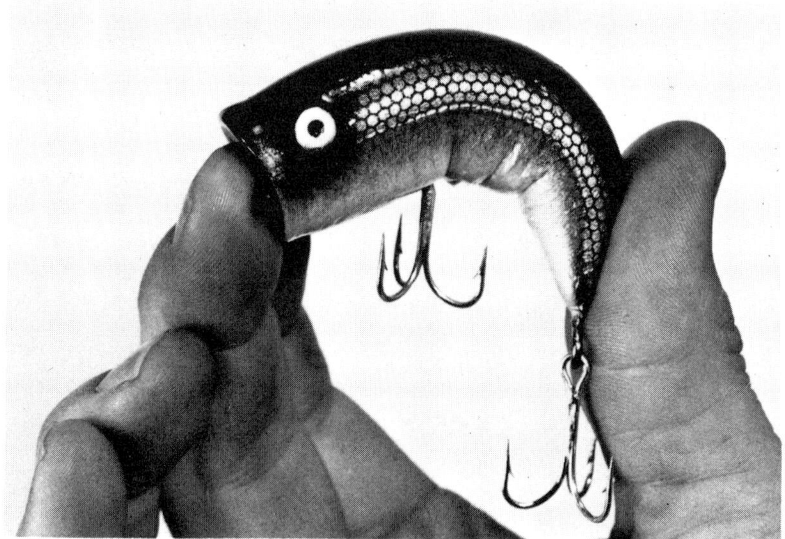

A few companies make lures of soft plastic. With these you get the benefits of natural feel and casting weight.

think about it, that you can only fish one depth with a bobber set one way. Without the bobber you can cast the minnow into very shallow water, allow him to sink to the bottom and then slowly reel back toward the boat, pulling the minnow into ever deepening water. The reverse is true when fishing from shore. Sure, you'll get the hook and minnow hung up on bottom many times during a day of fishing and have to break it off but all you are risking is a few pennies for split shot and hooks. When fishing from a boat you can motor over to the spot where the minnow is hung up and usually get the hook and shot free of the bottom. This is seldom possible when fishing from shore.

Modern Black Bass Fishing

In the last few years anglers have learned more about the proper way to go about black bass fishing than was learned in several preceeding decades. These advances have come partly from anglers themselves and partly from modern equipment that allows bass anglers to offer new forms of lures. Probably the most significant thing was the advent of the availability of soft plastic for lures. In any tackle store today you will find hundreds of different shapes, sizes and wildly-colored plastic worms and other forms of soft lures. It is very possible for an angler after black bass to specialize in fishing with these very effective plastic and rubber worm lures and never by any other type of lure or bait. I'm firmly convinced that following this system you would probably do about as well as anglers who use hundreds of different model lures. However, I personally own and use lures that fill three of the largest tackle boxes on the market. You and your youngster will have to decide whether to try a variety of lures or use only plastic worms.

You have to make one big concession when using plastic worms. One reason for their effectiveness is that they are always fished directly on the bottom. This means that regardless of how weedless and snag-free the hook is made you will always be hanging up on bottom. Most modern-day reservoirs were flooded in areas with tree stumps and the remains of brush. So, unlike natural lakes, the bottom of an artificial reservoir is almost always lined with things to snag lures on. And, because you can be certain you will be hanging up on the bottom when fishing with leadheads and plastic worms, you must plan for it. The best way to stop losing a lot of equipment is to buy an extra spool for your open-face spinning reel and fill it with much heavier line than is normally used for black bass fishing. (I use 15 and even 20-pound test monofilament for my own fishing.) You don't need line this heavy to capture the bass. Rather, you need it to avoid losing many dollars-worth of lures.

Fishing with lines as heavy as 15 or 20-pound test differs from fishing with lighter lines. The heavier material does not handle nearly as well. Line left on the spool between trips becomes stiff and wiry; in fact, it seems to have a life of its own when you try to cast it. The weights used for lines this heavy almost always have to be at least a half-ounce and weights close to an ounce handle even better. Most lures weigh from one-fourth to five-eighths of an ounce so most of them cannot be fished properly on the spool meant for worm or jig fishing. When I buy my heavy line for worm and jig fishing I buy the quarter-pound spools, which usually cost the same as quarter-pound spools of line of any size. There's no sense trying to conserve line by leaving it on a larger spool because the monofilament will take a curly set on a bulk spool just as fast as it will on the reel spool. It's so cheap at any rate that, even if you strip the spool and put on fresh line for each trip, you are only talking about a matter of a few pennies per trip. The added convenience of having limber, heavy line is certainly worth a cost like this.

Lures For Bottom Fishing

The key to success with any lure meant to be fished deep is to allow the lure to actually come into contact with the bottom. I use many different bottom type lures but they are always fished about the same. Probably the most popular bottom lure on the market today is the leadhead jig and combination leadhead and plastic worm. Any of these that strike your fancy will do a good job. It's strictly a matter of personal preference.

Although weights and lures that have the weight as an integral part of the hook can be used in plastic worm fishing, the rig I use more than any other is shown in the photograph. It is a simple cone-shaped sinker of about one-half to three-quarters of an ounce. The sinker has a hole down the center. The line is threaded through this hole and tied to a weedless hook of large size. The reason the hook is called weedless is that it has a stiff wire tied just behind the eye of the hook that extends down over the point of the hook. This hook is not 100 percent weedless but it is as nearly snag-free as any hook on the market. The rubber or plastic worm (there are literally thousands of different types and colors to choose from) is threaded onto the hook so that the front end of the worm comes up exactly to the inside of the hook eye. Hook size is determined by the size of the worm you are going to use: a very small worm should have a relatively small hook and a large one a large hook. In any case the hook should be large

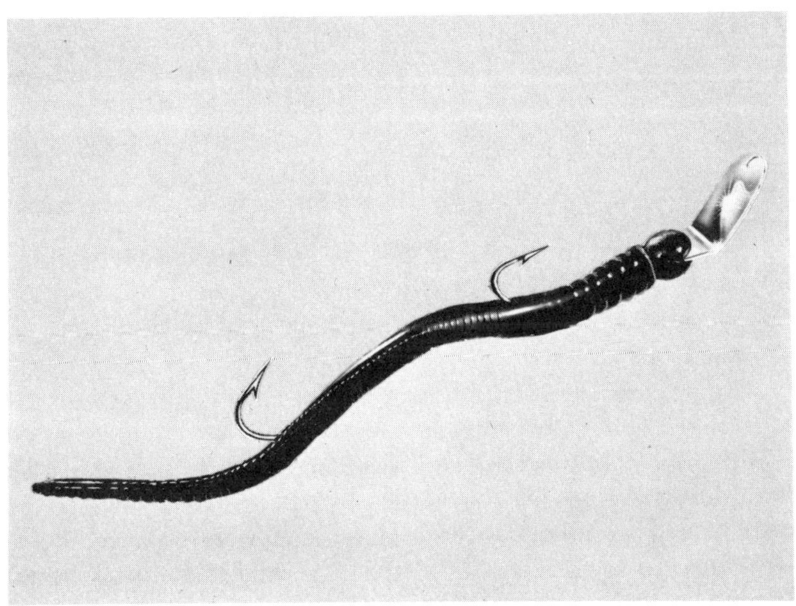

This jig and plastic worm has a wiggling disk at the front to give action when it is reeled back in.

enough to leave plenty of bend showing outside the threaded plastic worm to hook over the lip of a bass.

Even with 15 or 20-pound test monofilament a plastic worm rigged with a weight of almost an ounce can be easily cast by adults or youngsters.

Fishing With Plastic Worms

Using this type of lure is simplicity itself. If you are fishing from shore merely cast out into deep water and allow it to sink, with the bail open, until it rests on the bottom. I generally allow it to sit on bottom for a period of time before I raise the rod tip and begin to reel very slowly back toward shore. Actually experimentation pays off in this sort of fishing. Allowing the lure to rest on bottom for at least 30 seconds is usually best. Sometimes I find these lures are most effective if they are reeled slowly and steadily back to the rod tip. Just as often a hop and retrieve, then pause retrieve is better. I've also had days when a fast retrieve excited bass, although this happens infrequently in most lakes. It is impossible to fish worm lures too slow. In fishing from a boat the only difference is that you allow the boat to drift a fair casting distance offshore while you cast the worms in toward shore. Generally, it's not a good idea to anchor in bass fishing. In fact, I rarely even turn off the motor when I'm bass fishing. I've never found it made much difference to the fish. They are used to constant boating on most of our well-fished lakes and don't seem to associate the vibrations of a passing or stationary boat with danger of any kind.

Other Lures For Bass

Although plastic worms and leadhead jigs are probably the most effective lures for the sophisticated bass in our lakes, few anglers will want to fish with them exclusively. Personally I look forward to those times of the year when bass are willing to chase a lure at or near the surface. There is nothing quite like the thrill of seeing a big bass smash a lure worked right on the surface.

When you enter a tackle shop you will see literally hundreds of different lures, lure models and lure sizes. It might seem an overwhelming problem to make a choice from stacks and stacks of lures. There's no need to worry too much. There are only a few *types* of lures.

There are floating lures, floating lures that dive when retrieved, and sinking lures that do not float at all. It's as simple as that. Just check the box to find out which type of lure it contains and buy a few of each type rather than many of one type. The first lures in any collection should be around a half-ounce in weight. This size casts best with lines that test 10 or 12 pounds, the size line that should be used for most casting with average lures. Other lures can be added to the collection as time goes along. Most fishermen will stop at a tackle store where they are going to fish and buy a few lures recommended for that particular body of water. The prices are usually inflated right at the fishing site but generally the tackle merchant will suggest lures local anglers use successfully because he knows that if you take fish you'll be back.

How To Use Lures

How lures should be used to fish any given set of circumstances is actually the art of fishing for any species. What is said here applies to any species of gamefish. Under no circumstances could I possibly detail all the situations possible during even one day of fishing in any lake or stream. However, there should be a definite pattern to fishing most situations. Like most fishermen who have been fishing for many years I have a huge assortment of lures, from tiny ones to large and gaudy ones. A beginner will be fishing with only a few but should still have the three basic types, which, if used properly will allow him to take about as many fish as the angler with hundreds or even thousands of lures.

In my own fishing I usually try to get on the water before the sun has hit the surface. The hours around dawn and the few hours before dusk are very important in fishing. The normal pattern of all fish, and especially gamefish, is to move into the shallower sections of a lake or stream during these hours of light change. There are several explanations for this behavior. First of all, fish have no eyelids. Therefore they seek shade or deeper water during the sun-bright hours of each day. Also, they find the food they seek in shallower water where the sun can penetrate to the bottom and cause plant and animal growth. So if you and your youngster can get to the water at an early hour in a fishing day very probably your best bet would be to move along shore in a boat or on foot and fish very near the shoreline.

As the day wears on most gamefish will move into deeper water where they find relief from sunlight and the safety of deeper water. So, as the fishing day progresses you should begin to fish in ever deeper water, up to about 40 feet in the majority of lakes. This applies to all gamefish. In the afternoon or near dusk, when they will usually begin moving into shallow water again in order to feed, start fishing closer in to shore again.

If I am in a boat, which I generally am, I usually work my way slowly along the shore a comfortable casting distance from the shore. I alternately put the boat into gear and take it

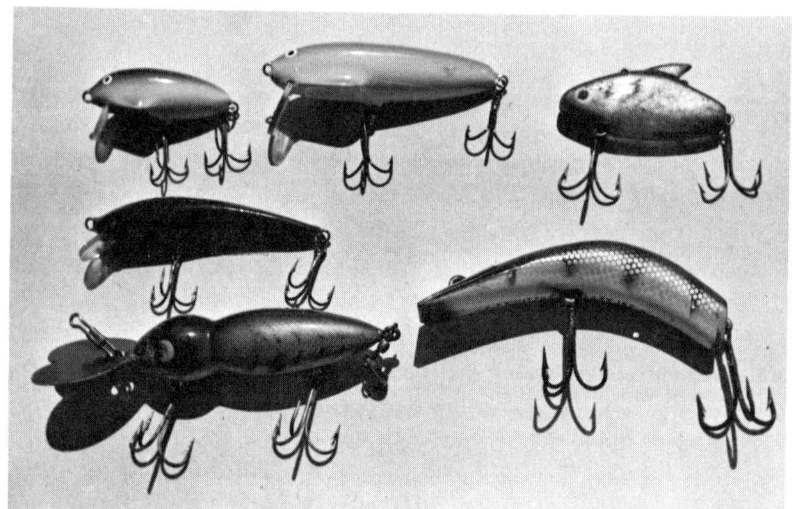

A selection of floating, diving and sinking lures. The thing to strive for in a lure collection is variety, so even the novice should have at least a few of each type.

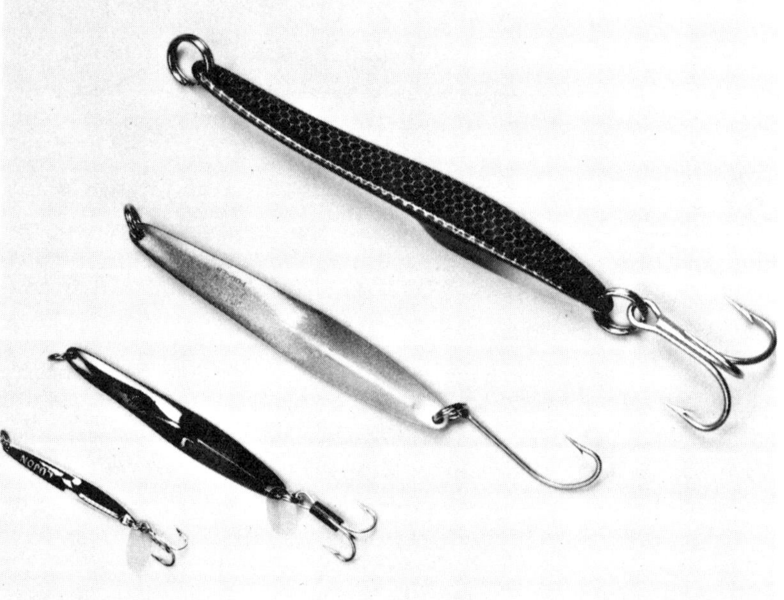

These lures can be used in both trolling and casting. They can be used in fresh or saltwater, although they are normally associated with saltwater sport.

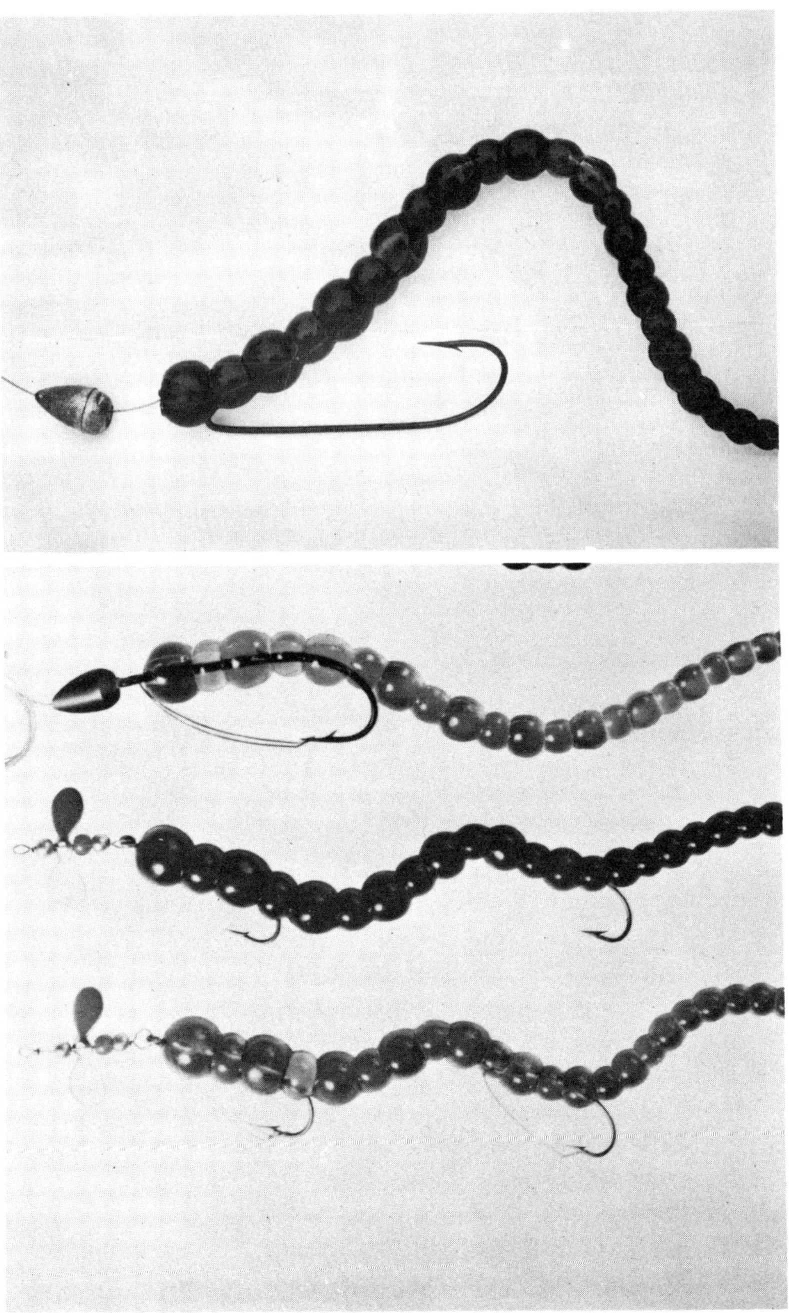

Some variations on rigging a worm.

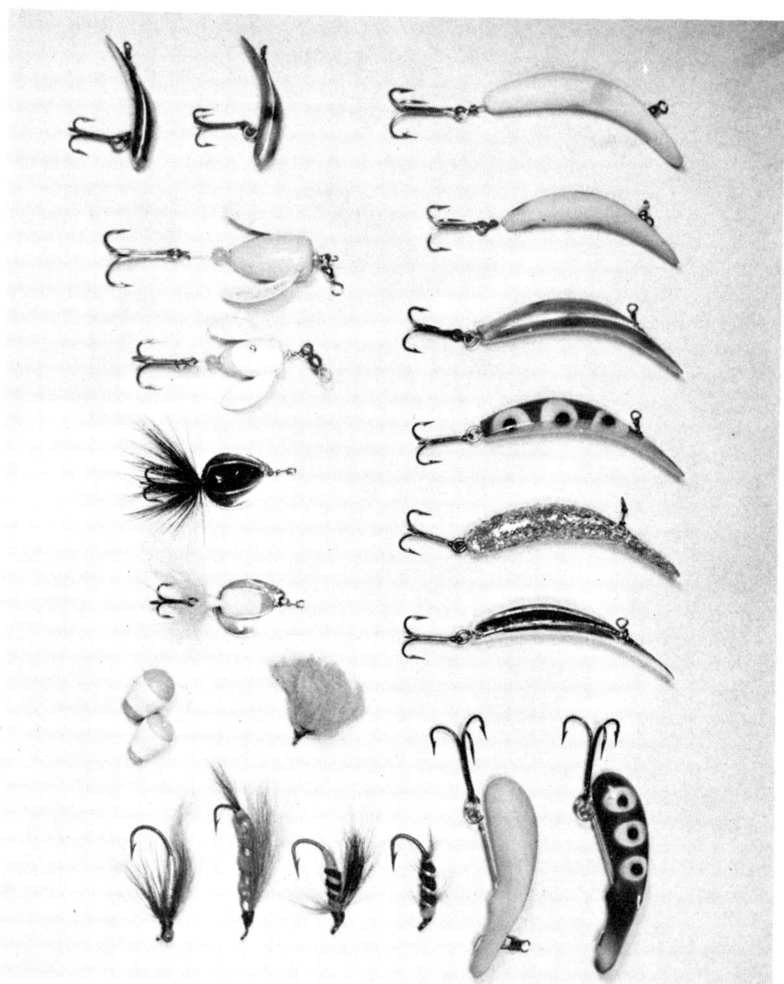

A selection of lures and flies that are normally associated with trolling. Most need additional weight added to the line in order to get casting weight.

out in order to fish interesting sections of the shore. An area with good brush or rock cover is nearly always worth fishing carefully. After you both become proficient at casting it is even possible to fish along a shore without ever taking the boat out of gear. I usually put the boat into reverse and slowly work my way down a shoreline, casting repeatedly to the actual shoreline, as well as to obstructions and brush or weeds. Each angler in the boat should start off using a different type of lure. The reason for this is that you are trying to determine which *type* of lure is most effective for that particular day of fishing in that particular body of water.

In the literature of angling you will find many mentions of lure color. Color definitely does affect a fish's preference in lures but it seems no two writers or fishermen can make up their minds about which colors are the right ones to use. I'm tempted to say that I pay little or no attention to the color of the lures I am using but I have to admit I'm partial to colors like red, yellow and black for bass fishing and silver and brass for trout fishing.

The speed at which you retrieve a lure can also be an important factor. In the vast majority of cases I have found that the more slowly a lure is worked the more productive it is. This is true with nearly any type of lure. There are rare occasions when a fast-moving lure is more productive; so if fish aren't responding to slow or moderate retrieves, then try a few fast retrieves. With lures like surface poppers I have found it best to cast the lure to the shore or near a drowned object and allow all the ripples to vanish before the lure is popped. Actually the term popper can be very confusing. Usually the most successful way to fish these lures on a calm surface is to move the line just enough to cause the lure to disturb the surface. At most, I usually move them only enough to cause them to make a modest "blooping" sound. I've also found that well over 90 percent of all the fish taken with surface poppers or wounded minnow imitations will be caught within the first two or three feet of retrieve. Because of this habitual behavior, I just work the lure the first few feet, then reel it in faster.

Trolling For Trout

Trolling consists of drawing a line through the water behind a moving boat. It is not much practiced when fishing for bass. Slow trolling can be helpful in trying to locate concentrations of some species, such as crappie and white bass. But trolling is probably the most important way of taking trout in a lake. Most anglers are far too haphazard in the way they go about their trolling. Trolling should have a very definite pattern.

Trout are not usually considered bottom-dwelling fish like black bass. However I have found that trout do patrol around in a lake in a very definite pattern that has a relationship to the bottom structure of the lake. I have electronic equipment that allows me to see how this pattern develops on the scope. Usually the trout will swim along slowly from three to perhaps 12 feet above the bottom in water shallower than 40 feet. In very deep water trout are generally found at 40 to 70 foot depths, rarely much deeper. With the equipment used by informed anglers today, it is possible to fish almost any depth for trout, or the mixed trout and salmon populations found in many lakes today.

Actively feeding trout will usually be found in water from about 45 to 55 degrees in temperature. For my own trolling I generally spend some time early in the day checking the temperature of the lake water with a depth thermometer. They cost only a few dollars but I hardly think you will want to purchase one very early in your fishing. Instead you can make a simple check of water temperature by merely putting your hand in the water. If you are fishing at very high altitudes, you will probably find, even during hot summer months, that water close to the surface is cold enough to contain trout. At lower elevations, however, it is probably useless to try fishing close to the surface, even at dawn and dusk, because it is very unlikely trout will be in the relatively warm shallow water.

Trolling Methods

There are two schools of thought about trolling for trout in a lake. One school uses relatively heavy rods and fishes with flashers, combined with lures or baits. The flasher has a series of spinner blades strung on a piece of wire that whirl as they are drawn through the water. The line is tied to the front end of the flasher wire. The lure, or bait, is attached to the end of a four or five-foot piece of monofilament line, called a leader.

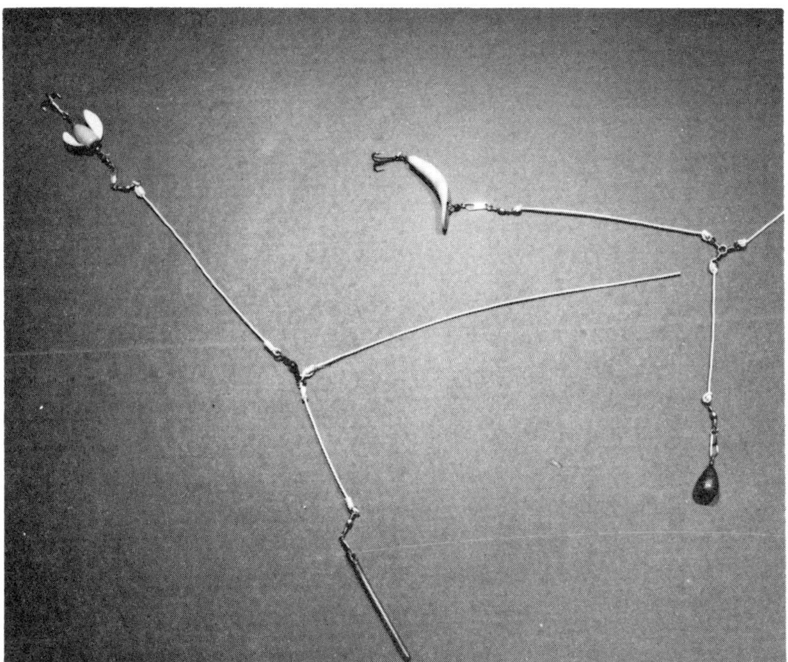

These are good trolling rigs.

Because of the drag of the spinners, plus lure or bait, heavy rods and reels are necessary in this sort of fishing. I do not like this kind of fishing because even large trout cannot possibly show what they can do when they are pitted against heavy equipment and impeded by the drag of the spinner blades as they try to escape. Instead, I go along with the second school of thought and use very light lines and work with a different approach. I've never found it necessary to use flasher blades on any fish except kokanee salmon, which are found in many lakes throughout the country.

The way I rig for trout fishing in a lake is to start with four-pound test monofilament. I tie on a big snap swivel about three or four feet up the line from the end. It is important that the snap swivel be large enough to accommodate several fairly large sinkers. A small one cannot do this. If I am fishing at very high elevation, or at a time of year where the water near the surface of a lake is cool enough so it might contain trout, I tie on a small lure (a wobbling spoon or any lure suitable for trout) and hang a small weight of maybe a half-ounce on the line. Rigged like this the lure will usually run less than 10-feet deep. It is important at this point to make sure you keep track of every element of trolling. It really doesn't matter very much what kind of lure you are using but knowing what the lure is doing is all important to consistent success.

You do not merely cast the lure out and begin to troll. Instead, click off the anti-reverse lever on the reel and count the number of revolutions as the lure trails out behind the boat. I usually stop the reel when it has made about 25 to 30 revolutions in reverse. If there are two rods in the boat they should be rigged differently. For instance a good combination is one rod fitted with a half-ounce sinker and the other with perhaps an ounce of weight. This way, with both lures out the same distance behind the boat, the half-ounce rig will probably be working at about an eight-feet depth and the other at perhaps 12 feet. This difference can be critical. Also, each rod should have a different type lure on it. This way you offer the fish a choice.

Trolling speed should be varied. Generally the faster you move the boat the shallower the lures will be running. This is because of the drag of the water against the line, which tends to plane the lures toward the surface. I usually start trolling about as slowly as the motor will turn over in order to get the lure down deep as possible.

With any given combinations of weight, motor speed and lure I generally will allow perhaps 10 or 15 minutes without a strike before I make a change. If I go this long without a strike I will let the spool out perhaps five or 10 more revolutions for another 10 or 15 minutes. The other rod should also be changed at these intervals. It really doesn't matter how much line or what kind of rigging you've got on either rod but be sure to keep track of exactly how you are trolling. Sometimes it takes hours and many changes before you manage to hook a fish. (I usually limit this kind of fishing to a maximum of five or six ounces of weight—any more and you are defeating the purpose of using light trolling equipment.) If you do manage

A cartop boat is ideal for trolling, as well as most fishing in lakes and bays. A small boat like this can be put into the water nearly anywhere, unlike the trailer-hauled boat which needs a launching site.

to hook a fish, and have kept track of line length, lure type and amount of weight it is relatively easy to return to that combination with both rods and very probably take a lot of trout. If you don't keep track of every element you have to start all over again.

You should try to be as observant of everything you are doing while trolling. I have seen very small items make a big difference in the number of trout hooked. Sometimes you will only take trout while going upwind. This is because of the slight difference in the speed of the boat going into the wind and on the downwind leg of a troll, which controls how deep the lure is running. I've seen cases where the only time you hook a trout is when you are making a turn. Again the effect of water drag on lure depth is the cause. This is so critical that sometimes only the rod on the inside of the turn, moving a bit slower than the rod on the outside, will take a fish. When really slow trolling is necessary I even put the boat in reverse and troll. This lets the boat move as slowly as possible and allows you to get maximum depths with the lure. You should also keep track of exactly where you are taking your trout. Trout in a big lake behave in specific patterns. Often you'll find you only hook a fish when you pass over a point of land jutting out into the lake. If you begin to hook trout in a certain spot, locate landmarks on the shore in four directions 180 degrees from each other so you can return to the exact spot again.

Considering all the factors in this trial-and-error method, it's no wonder that it often takes many hours or even days to locate the exact formula for taking trout when trolling a specific lake. But usually when you finally do figure out the exact combination it is possible to take a limit or a good number of trout in very short order. Very few kids have the patience to sit out the preliminary period, so it just might be a good idea to have the adult or adults do the searching part of trolling. Then when the right combination is figured out the youngster can come along for the exciting part of the fishing trip: catching the fish. The same applies to stream or bay and ocean fishing where there's a chance you are going to have to spend a long period of time doping out the right way to take fish. Figuring out how to take fish in each new situation is actually what fishing is all about and anyone with many years of experience likes this part of the sport. But a nicety like this is usually lost on a kid who is there for the action not for the mental gymnastics involved in doping out every new situation. Of course all youngsters are not the same and the decision whether or not to include them in the duller parts of trolling and learning has to be made by the interested adult.

STREAM FISHING

In the vast majority of situations, stream fishing is the most demanding kind of fishing for the beginning angler. This is particularly true if the stream is a small one. A possible exception would be in the case where a stream had been freshly stocked with catchable trout by the fish and game agency. Usually these smaller trout are very easy for anyone to catch and are worth consideration for the first few trips.

The main difficulty faced by the beginner in stream fishing is manipulating equipment while confronted by many obstacles, rather than any reluctance of gamefish to take the angler's offering. Almost all streams have rocks, snags and other obstructions in the main flow and the successful angler is the one who manages to place his bait or lures in the area directly behind these obstacles. This is where fish lie waiting for the current to bring them a supply of food. This is true for trout, panfish, and other gamefish like black bass, which are found in streams in most parts of the country. Another set of obstacles

The angler who fishes a great deal will need many different types of equipment. Even though equipment may seem costly, it is about the cheapest part of fishing.

is usually found along brush-lined banks of most streams. Often this brush is so thick an angler has to be very accomplished with his tackle just to make reasonably effective casts.

Types of Streams

Naturally streams come in all shapes and sizes. In many areas there are a variety from which to chose, from tiny brooks up to huge rivers. As a general rule it is best to select the larger streams for the first few stream-fishing efforts. Normally, a large stream will offer a much larger selection of fish, in contrast to the more specialized fishing in smaller streams. In addition, the very size of a larger stream usually makes it easier to fish because the depth and flow is so much greater.

When fishing a brook the angler has to be much more careful with his streamside approach. Fish in small streams survive primarily because they are very cautious, unlike the large stream fish which are subject to less intense predatory action by land animals. Another reason to avoid small streams on the first few trips is the delicacy needed to make accurate casts when presenting lures or baits to fish. Often large sections of a small brook will be completely overgrown by brush and reeds along the banks, or even form a tunnel of trees and brush completely covering the area over the stream. It can be exciting and intimate fishing to work a lure or bait in a small brook setting but usually it is best to wait until the youngster and adult have had many fishing trips before attempting this demanding kind of fishing. As a general rule I think the best selection for the first few stream fishing trips would be a moderate-size stream that is reasonably free of streambed obstructions, providing you have a selection of different streams in the area you are going to try. The ideal situation would be to find a stream that can be covered with your best casts to within a short distance of the far side. A cast made to the far side of a stream is called a "quartering" cast.

Fishing Stream Basics

Regardless of the size of a stream you are going to fish, there are certain basics that never vary much. Fish will rarely hold in areas where the water is flowing constantly or fast. In the case of trout, certain sections of a stream that look on the surface to be very fast-flowing may contain trout. This is particularly true of rainbow, brook and cutthroat trout. But an experienced angler knows that even though the flow of water looks rapid from the surface, if it is to contain trout there must be a depression in the bottom, a hidden boulder to break up the flow of the current or some other kind of obstruction mostly hidden from view at the surface. No trout or other kind of fish can survive long in an area where they must constantly battle the force of a heavy current.

When experienced anglers speak about fishing any part of a stream they will say that you have to be able to "read" a section of stream in order to be successful. What they mean by this is that through past experience they are able to tell, merely by looking at the flow of water and the many swirls and side currents in the flow, just where gamefish or panfish *should* be holding. One of the things that makes stream fishing so interesting is that there are so many variations of current and obstructions to be figured out by the serious fisherman. However, this works to the disadvantage of the beginner because he doesn't haave a collective bank of experience to draw on when he faces each new situation. A beginner at stream fishing may well spend most of his time fishing areas that very probably do not have any chance of holding fish. If you understand a few of the basics of stream fishing you can offset much of the disadvantage of lack of experience.

Fish The Edges

Many anglers fish their entire lives without realizing that panfish and gamefish are creatures that frequent the "edges" of their watery environment. In a lake this is relatively easy to understand because gamefish skirt the edges of the lake, the edges of dropoffs into deep water and even the "edge" of the surface. For every fish you find swimming at random in the mid-depths of a lake there will be many more feeding and swimming just off the surface, sides and bottom. In stream fishing exactly the same thing applies, except it is a bit more complicated and difficult to determine where the edges are in a flowing body of water.

As water moves down the length of any kind of stream it flows against the sides and over and around many obstructions. When the stream flows into an underwater obstruction —say a rock or fallen tree—there is a small area in front of the obstruction and a larger one behind where the characteristics of the water change. Directly in front of an obstruction in a moderately flowing stream there is a cushioning effect in the flow and directly behind the obstruction the flow of the current is stopped almost completely as the water swirls around the obstruction to form a "pocket" of water. These areas are very attractive to fish because they can swim in the area where they find relief from the flow of the stream and still watch the current for food.

As stream current moves down the channel of a river or stream the friction of the moving water causes the current to slow where it comes into contact with the bottom and sides. Fish find refuge from the effects of the current in any spot where there is the slightest obstruction, such as a boulder or root structure jutting out from the sides and bottom. As the water is deflected away from the bottom in these areas a small pocket of almost non-flowing water is formed. Naturally these hidden obstructions are far more difficult to detect than the larger pockets behind boulders and snags visible at the surface. A very experienced angler can detect these hidden obstructions by noting where the water swirls back on itself. In fact, you should carefully note any kind of change in the flow pattern because a swirl or change in the straight flow of the stream is a clue to hidden fish-holding areas.

As a stream twists and winds down its length, the action of the current will dig earth and smaller stones from the bank and bottom. Anywhere there are stream obstructions that cause the stream to flow over rocks or trees the current will eventually dig out a pocket of deeper water where it falls on the downstream side of the obstruction. These are called pocket falls by anglers. They can be very large where the fall of water is great and very small where there is a more gentle fall of water. Further complications to flow patterns are often caused by additional obstructions within the larger fall pocket, which trap other obstructions such as drowned or floating logs, all of which provide ideal holding water for fish.

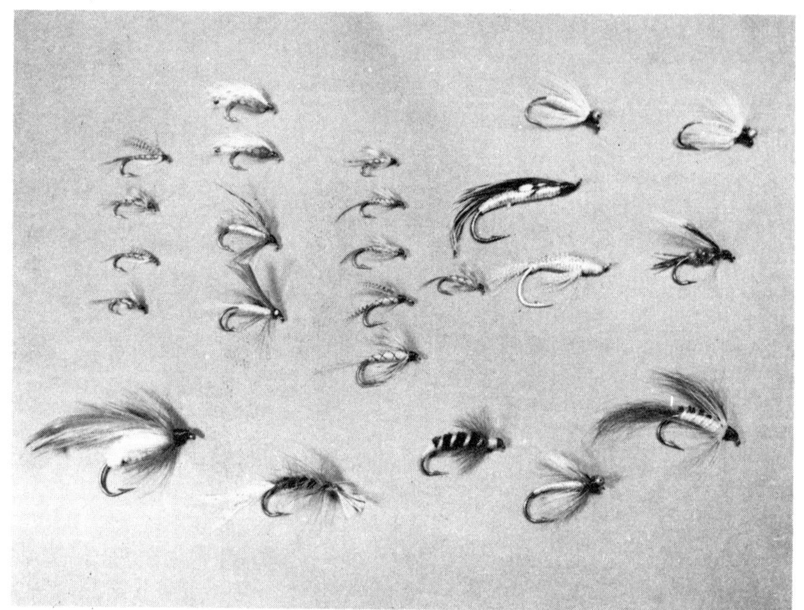

A sinking fly selection. Note the variety of size and shading.

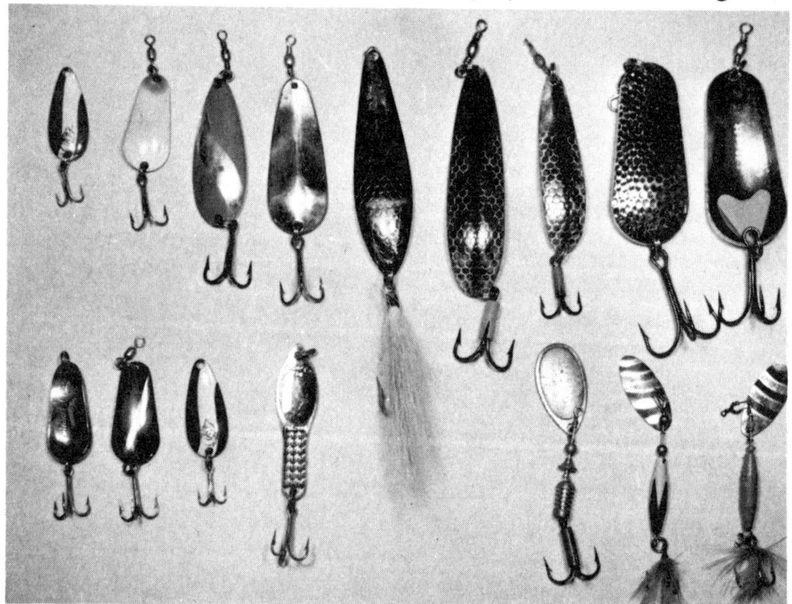

Metal lures are a good choice to start a day of fishing because no additional weight is needed to get casting weight. They are the simplest of all types of lures to use.

If the stream you have chosen flows through meadow or pasture land you will find the force of the current has caused the banks to erode to form undercut banks. In many cases the earth, filled with grass and brush roots, is firm enough at the surface so that the undercut part of the bank is very extensive. Most meadow streams meander through the soft earth rather than flow in a straight line. As willows and other streamside brush form on the banks they firm up the earth even more and trail their branches down into the water. This is attractive to fish of all kinds because the undercut bank and the trailing "sweepers" of brush provide escape from direct sunlight and protection from natural predators. The fish will hold well back under these undercut banks during the brighter hours of the day where they can feel secure and still be in position to dart out into the main flow of the stream to feed. The main problem the fisherman faces in fishing this sort of stream is being able to approach likely spots along the undercut banks without scaring the fish. Generally, a meadow stream with undercut banks is particularly spongy and soft to walk on. As the angler moves down the bank his footsteps create vibrations in the earth that are detected instantly by a fish holding in the undercut. This makes for interesting fishing but it also puts a premium on the amount of stealth an angler can accomplish. A beginner, particularly a kid, may not understand the need for creeping along this kind of bank in order to get into position to cast accurately to within inches of the banks, but it is all important when fishing a meadow stream. In fact, serious fishermen even claim it is necessary to crawl on their hands and knees to get into position to make an offering to fish in most meadow water. I have often said I wear the knees out of my wading equipment before I wear out the soles.

It can be very frustrating to a youngster (or an adult, for that matter) to see fish rising to the surface of a placid meadow stream, only to have them stop feeding and go into hiding as they approach. This is one reason this kind of water should be avoided until the fisherman has had more experience in stream fishing. In fact, if you have a choice between two streams or two sections of the same stream with one offering meadow water, the other pocket water broken up with many obstructions, chose the one with the broken pocket water. At the very least, you will eliminate the problems faced with a stealthy approach. In broken pocket water you still have to be fairly careful but it is not anything like the approach problem faced in calm, clear meadow sections of a stream.

Fishing The Average Stream

For our purposes here we'll term a stream as average if you can cast with your best cast to the far bank or perhaps a bit beyond. This is the ideal stream to use for the first few stream fishing trips. Of course, it's a relatively rare situation to find a stream of exactly the right size, but most of what we say here would hold even if the stream being fished were a very large one.

Upon approaching any stream your first move should be to stop and "size up" the stream. This is merely a moment or two spent looking at the stream. I generally suggest that an angler make this pause some distance away from the actual bank. The reason for this is so you will have a chance to check for holes, rocks, logs or other obstructions that may have fish before you actually reach the bank. If you walk right up to the bank you may scare fish that are holding on the near side of the stream, close to the bank you will fish from. In all stream fishing you have to realize there are probably just as many fish near your side of the stream as near the other. Many anglers do not seem to realize this and are forever trying to make long casts to the far side of a stream before they thoroughly fish the near side. The ideal place to size-up any stream is from a spot higher than the actual surface of the water. Often, with careful observation you can actually see fish in the stream. In addition, most species of gamefish and panfish found in streams will often give an indication of where they are holding and feeding by showing at the surface. This is what anglers are referring to when they say they were on the stream when fish (usually trout) were "rising". This occurs when fish are feeding on insects floating on or very near the surface.

If you are fortunate enough to arrive at the stream, or are fishing the stream, when there is an active rise, by all means try to determine exactly what it is the fish are feeding on. Normally you can do this by just closely watching the nearby surface to see what type of insect is floating past. Once you determine the kind of insect you should attempt to "match the hatch," as anglers call this identification. An angler with a lot of experience and lots of flies in different sizes and colors can quickly select a certain fly that comes close to imitating the insect on the stream surface. A beginner, naturally, would not have this many flies. But a beginner should have at least a few flies in his equipment collection for just such situations. First try to match the insect in the matter of size. To fish size is more important than color, though color is definitely a factor when fish are feeding selectively and should be the second thing you try to match. You can use either a floating lure as a casting weight and tie the fly on with a short dropper strand a foot or so up the line, or you can use a standard plastic casting bubble for casting weight.

If you watch an active rise on a stream carefully you will see it is not a helter-skelter affair. Actively feeding fish seem to take up a station in the stream flow and feed in a definite pattern. For instance, a specific fish may station itself just out from a rock, log or some other form of shelter. It will hold near the surface and dart out to take any insect that floats past within a certain area, rarely more than a few feet away. Other fish will be doing the same thing in other parts of the stream. What you want to do in a situation like this is watch patiently until you can see exactly what the pattern is for each fish within your range of vision. It is almost always better to work upstream of the fish in this kind of situation, and also approach from one side. When fish are holding fairly near the surface they cannot see well to the rear so this is the place you want to make your first careful cast from.

Do not cast your lure directly to the spot where the fish is rising. Instead, try to make an accurate cast several feet in front of that spot, where the current will float the lure into the area where the fish is feeding. As I indicated, the area where an individual fish is surfacing is never very large, so your casts have to be accurate if you are going to get a perfect "drift," the fisherman's word for the floating distance between the fish and the place where you make your presentation cast. With wary gamefish it is often critical not to alarm an individual fish. In a clear, relatively sedate flowing stream a single frightened fish can alarm dozens of others. So, when you are making your size-up of the rise, be sure to try for the fish closest to the spot where you are standing before you try for those further away. Normally if you cast even the smallest lure or plastic float over the exact position of any fish in calm water you will frighten it enough to make it stop feeding actively. The proper way to fish a rise is to cast to the closest fish first, until you have either caught him or disturbed him enough so he has quit feeding, then to others further away.

If you make two or three casts to a specific fish that are accurate enough to make you relatively positive the fish has at least seen your offering, and he still doesn't respond, change the offering. Again, the most important thing is to change the size of the offering rather than to worry much about the color. Continue to change the fly or lure every time you don't tempt a fish within two or three accurate casts. In this situation, naturally, you cannot count those casts that are not accurate or that don't drift into the cone of vision of the feeding fish.

Most of this lore concerning fishing a hatch concerns cold-water fish like trout. However, smallmouth and largemouth bass and almost all of the panfish species will act exactly the same way when they are feeding on insects. The main difference is where bass or panfish will be holding in a stream. As a general rule, panfish in a given stream will be holding in the very calmest water they can find. In fact, they usually prefer nearly still water. Largemouth bass will rarely tolerate water that has more than a very modest current. Smallmouth bass will be found in still water, usually in pockets behind an obstruction, but they are willing to dart out into relatively fast-flowing water to take a bait or lure. Sometimes, in very clear water you can actually see this difference in the various species and which sections of the stream each kind of fish prefer. This is good information to remember if you are fishing

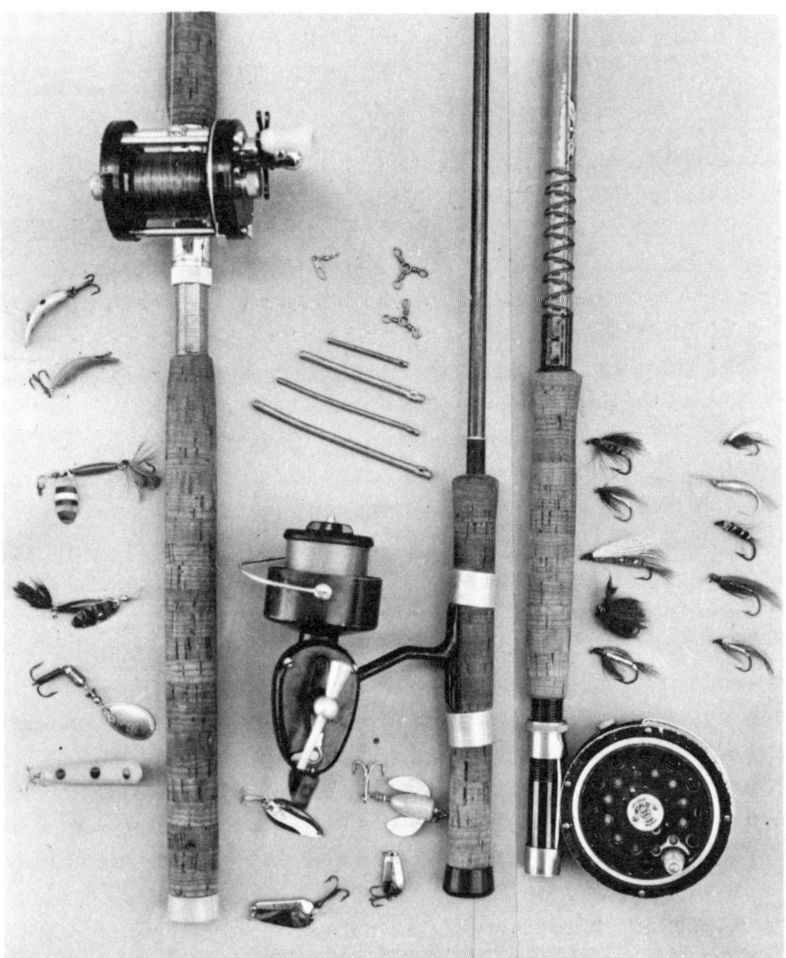

There are three general types of fly-fishing equipment used by the majority of fishermen. The spinning outfit in the middle here is best suited for most angling done by beginners and youngsters.

the same stream when there is no rise or when the water is discolored by rains or natural discoloration. Storing this kind of information in your memory bank will eventually determine how consistently successful you will be in all of your fishing. The more times you go on a stream and the more times you discover where the fish are holding and what kind of lures and bait each prefer, the better your chances.

Set Up a Pattern

An experienced angler can approach any stream and automatically exclude about 90 percent of all the water. The reason he doesn't need to fish every bit of the water is that past experience has informed him just where the fish hold. A beginner doesn't have this ability to read the water accurately so he has to fish most of the water. It is not productive to merely begin casting at random. You should set up a regular pattern in stream fishing.

The simplest pattern is to cast a series of arcs. The reason I say arcs is because this is how the lure or bait drifts, due to the action of a moving stream against it and the drag of the water against the line. The first few casts should be made from a position well back from the edge of the stream. The proper distance back from the stream edge should be determined by how well you can make the cast, while still being able to hold the line up high enough to clear any obstructions on the bank and still get a clean drift. On a sandbar, for example, it's possible to stand a good distance back from the edge and still get a good drift. When there are no fish visible, as is usually the situation, start casting across and slightly upstream from where you are standing. This is called "blind casting" or "blind drifting."

After you have made a few short casts upstream from well back on the bank, move up to the bank and make a few short casts straight across or slightly downstream. It is generally best to cast so the lure or bait passes close to any visible or indicated obstructions in the stream. You want your offering to pass as close to these obstructions as possible without getting hung up on them. After you have covered any nearby obstruction work your lure or bait farther out until you have worked all of them as far out as you can cast. You should also fish all obstructions and cross currents upstream from where you are standing. After you have covered all the water you can reach from that spot it's time to move a few paces down or upstream and repeat the series of casts to new water. Whether to move down or upstream is a matter of personal preference. If I am using lures I generally choose the downstream approach. Lures are easier to control when working against the current rather than with it flowing toward you. A lure such as a spinner, wobbler or plug will need the force of the current as well as the drag from the line being reeled in to make it have action, hence the downstream approach is usually best. On the other hand, if I am using flies or baits I usually will fish upstream. The drift of a fly or bait can be controlled by reeling faster or slower as it floats and drifts back toward you. Usually a fly or bait looks very unnatural if it is being dragged across the current. In any event, keep moving along the bank almost continually. In most cases you will either have taken any fish willing to take your offering or have alerted it to your presence within less than five minutes of casting in any given spot. The exception to this might be in the case of migrating fish like salmon, steelhead, shad or other fish that are moving upstream. However, I usually keep moving even when I am fishing for these migrating fish. While they are moving upstream, these fish have to pass through the entire stream anyway, so I feel you are not losing much by moving from one spot to another until you find a spot where there are willing fish.

The Drift

In stream fishing it is impossible to overemphasize the importance of understanding the mechanics of the drift. The number of things that have to be taken into consideration in drift fishing are so great the elements can almost be said to be infinite. Youngsters tend to have trouble keeping their minds on what they are doing when they fish a stream. This is particularly true of very young children. It is unfortunate that the very sections of streams that take the most attention to the mechanics of drift are also the most productive. A section of stream with a great number of obstructions will always produce the most fish per mile but they are difficult stretches for youngsters to fish precisely because of these obstructions. If you have a choice you should choose a section of stream that is relatively slow moving and mostly free of obstructions for the first trip. In a deep section of stream you have a much better chance to learn and teach the mechanics of drift fishing.

It is a good idea to check the stream's current and depth before the youngster joins you.

The first casts should be done with either a floating lure or a plastic casting float with bait or fly attached to a dropper strand about a foot up the line from the float. A dropper strand is just a length of monofilament line of a foot or two in length connecting the main line and bait or fly. Rigged this way you can easily determine the action and reaction of the float to the various currents. Since the float keeps the lure suspended in the water, you have the added advantage of not having to worry about getting a lure hung up on the bottom, unless the water is very shallow. With a visible float or lure you can see how the water current quickens as it meets an obstruction. Directly behind a visible obstruction you can see there is a swirl, or backwater where there is virtually no water movement. When the float passes a hidden obstacle under the surface there is a different kind of action, but basically the water swirls the same way it does when the obstruction is visible.

When you cast upstream you can find out the best way to reel in line and lift or lower the rod tip to make a lure or float match the currents. Usually this is the best way to fish either a bait or a fly because the current normally gives flies or baits all the action they need as they float back toward the caster. With a visible lure or float you can see how the action of the flowing water against the tight line causes it to return to the rod tip in a shallow arc downstream from the rod. This might seem simple to an adult but many youngsters have a difficult time envisioning this effect unless they can see it with their own eyes. In many cases it might be a good idea for the adult working with very young children to do the fishing until a fish is actually hooked. Then the youngster can take the rod and reel in the fish.

Each adult has to make an individual choice about how soon a given youngster can be introduced to fishing obstruction areas of the stream. There is every chance that most youngsters will get their lures and baits hung up in this kind of water. In fact, in fast-moving, relatively shallow sections of a stream you may spend most of your time breaking off snagged hooks and tying knots instead of fishing. The alternative is to find a deep section or a single deep hole and try still-fishing. Admittedly this is probably the poorest way to catch fish in a stream but often it is the only choice. If you are forced to do this be sure to move the bait often to give any available fish in the pool a chance to see the bait. If the stream has a lot of pools it's a good idea to move from one to another after still-fishing a single pool no more than a half hour, at most. If you decide to fish a section with white water indicating many obstructions it's a good idea to use the cheapest terminal rig you can find. If you hang up a single hook and a small weight you aren't out a lot of money. If you fish with expensive lures it can cost a great deal of money during even a single session of fishing, unless the youngster is very alert and capable with his equipment and understands how the currents act on a lure.

EXPANDING YOUR FISHING

Catching fish with spinning equipment is the most logical place to start enjoying fishing but once you've become a "Fishing Family" it is very reasonable to want to expand your fishing interests into other forms of the sport. As a family gains experience in fishing the areas available to them they will very probably become addicted to fishing for certain species of fish. For instance, in areas where the primary fish are the warm-water species such as black bass, a family could become deeply interested in taking more and larger bass. Any serious black bass fishermen will soon need to expand their use of equipment to include revolving spool or level-wind fishing equipment. If the family interest includes trout and most panfish species the need will be for a better understanding of the use of fly-fishing equipment. The better spinning outfits can be utilized in much of this fishing but to really excel at any of these specialized forms of fishing other types of equipment must be utilized. This might even be the case if you have decided that bait fishing is the way you like to fish. Then you will want to explore spin-casting equipment, even though it is harder to use, and line control is more difficult. But this method has applications, particularly in night fishing, that other equipment does not have.

Choosing the Next Form of Fishing

When your family arrives at the point of acquiring a specialized fishing interest, you must make a decision about the general type of equipment you would like. As a basic guide, if your interest is black bass, muskellunge or pike you should make your next equipment buy from the level-wind or revolving-spool group. If trout and panfish are your greatest interest fly-fishing equipment should be chosen. If you want to expand your saltwater fishing horizons either go into larger spinning equipment or to larger revolving-spool reels and surf-fishing gear that gives you the casting distances you will need for this kind of fishing.

By the time you are ready to expand into these other forms of fishing you will probably have learned there are fishermen who specialize in taking black bass with fly-rod equipment and there are fishermen who utilize special revolving-spool reels to take trout. There is nothing at all wrong with this if you decide this very specialized gear is for you; but you should keep in mind that these are very specialized systems of equipment and they have very definite limitations. A very good example of extremely specialized equipment is that used in saltwater fishing by fly fishermen. This can be and is a very exciting sport but the rods and lines used by these fishermen are so specialized they are effective for little else but saltwater fly fishing. They are virtually useless for trout fishing and even most fishing in lakes. Another example of extreme specialization in equipment is the extremely delicate level-wind gear. It is used with light monofilament lines and long rods for making very long casts in the estuary sections of salmon and steelhead streams along the coasts. By the time your family is ready to go into this kind of extremely specialized equipment you very probably will need no guidance other than your own experience.

SELECTING FLY FISHING EQUIPMENT

Fly fishing equipment is not really as difficult to learn to use as most people think, providing the basic components of rod, line and leader are all matched perfectly. Right at the start of learning fly casting you must thoroughly understand what makes this form of casting different from any other. In other types of casting you are utilizing a weight, in the form of a shaped lead sinker, a lure or bait. In fly fishing *the line is the weight.* It is easy to see how a shaped weight, bait or lure is used to gain the weight needed to pull the line from the spool. It is more difficult to understand the mechanics of weight when it is in a piece of thick line stretched out from 10 to 90 feet. But obviously if you merely lift a section of coiled fly line you will see that it does possess plenty of weight to make a good cast. If you merely tied the coiled line on your regular spinning outfit you could lob a very respectable cast with it.

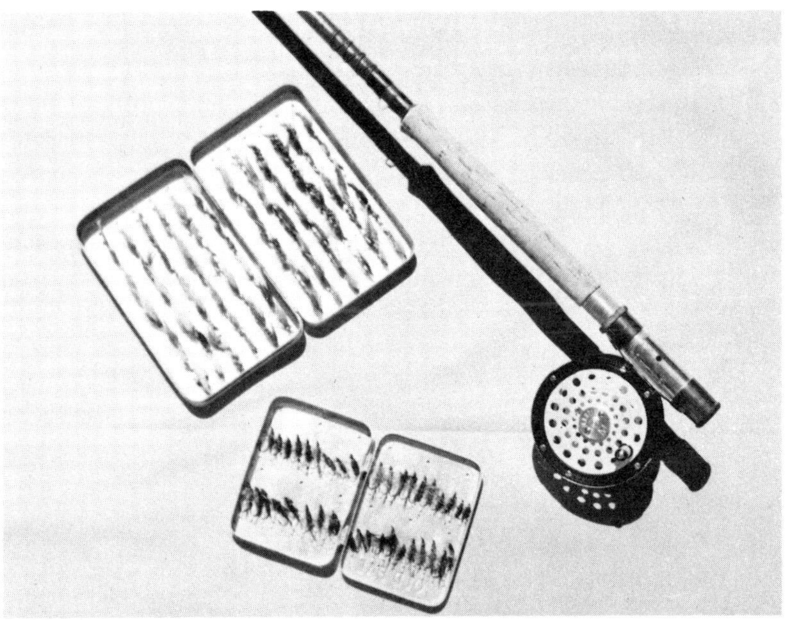

The necessities for successful fly fishing: a good light outfit that is comfortable to use and a fly box filled with a variety of different kinds of flies.

Matching Fly Equipment

The term "matching" when applied to fly fishing equipment is usually very confusing to anyone new to this form of sport fishing. Put most simply this means choosing a line that has enough weight in its first 30 feet (the part most used in fly casting) to bend the rod adequately so that a cast can be made with reasonable ease. It was once confusing to determine what all the numbers and letters meant when it came to matching a line, which could be made of many different materials possessing many different physical characteristics, to any given rod. Now a set of standards has been set up by the American Fishing Tackle Manufacturers Association to take some of the guesswork out of the problem. The main consideration of line selection is how much it weighs rather than the other characteristics, so these standards concern themselves basically with line weight. But there are other considerations, including shape (level, double taper, weight forward or single taper) and sinking or floating characteristics (such as floating, sinking and intermediate). Individual manufacturers have ways of further clarifying (or confusing) these characteristics by designating particular lines by terms such as fast sinking, deep sinking, lead core, but these are usually specialized lines of little concern to the beginner at fly fishing. By the time you are ready for these lines you will know what you want from them.

Here are the AFTMA standards for fly lines as currently used today:

No.	Wt.	Range*
1	60	54- 66
2	80	74- 86
3	100	94-106
4	120	114-126
5	140	134-146
6	160	152-168
7	185	177-193
8	210	202-218
9	240	230-250
10	280	270-290
11	330	318-342
12	380	368-392

AFTMA Fly Line Symbols		AFTMA Fly Line Types	
L	=Level	F	=Floating
DT	=Double Taper	S	=Sinking
WF	=Weight Forward	I	=Intermediate (Float or Sink)
ST	=Single Taper		

*Manufacturing tolerances

Examples:

A line marked DT 6 F would be a double-taper line with the first 30 feet weighing between 152 and 168 grains and of the floating type. One marked L 9 S would be a sinking line weighing between 230 and 250 grains with a level shape.

If you're now thoroughly confused by the whole subject,

take my word for it, a double-taper dry fly-line is the best first choice.

Fly Rod Selection

Although the fly line is the most important element in selecting fly-fishing equipment the rod comes close to it in importance. And, while nearly any of the modern fiberglas rods will do a reasonable job of casting a fly line there are other basic elements to be taken into consideration. By the time you are ready to branch out into fly fishing, you probably will have realized that my statement about the cost of equipment being one of the minor expenses in the sport is true. This extends to purchasing fly equipment and is important when considering how much to spend for a fly rod. Even though a cheap rod will get the job done the more expensive fly rods come with much better fittings. An additional benefit is that most better fly rods come with information about which size fly line best fits them, either printed in a folder or right on the rod butt. This is a very important extra, especially for the beginner. These rods have been rated by experts at the factory and if you follow their directions you will always end up with a perfectly matched fly line and fly rod. In other words, these rod and line classifications take 100 percent of the guesswork out of matching a fly outfit. Another source of this kind of information is the line manufacturers. Most of the bigger companies print a list of the lines that match that major rods on the market. These lists normally do not include the so-called "drugstore fly rods."

The Fly Reel

The reel used to complete a fly rod outfit is the least important element in matching the components. In fly fishing the reel is used merely to store line between casting sessions. Some of the larger gamefish are fought from the reel but the majority of fish are brought in by stripping the line by hand. In selecting a reel for fly fishing choose the lightest one you can find. At one time angling writers and some fishermen believed the fly reel should be heavy enough to "balance" the outfit for better casting. Modern fishermen no longer subscribe to this idea. Fly reels are not complicated or expensive, in most cases you can get a very servicable fly reel for about $15 or less. Naturally the more you spend for the reel the longer you can expect it to give good service. Do not choose a reel that is either too big or too small for the rod you choose.

What Length Rod?

There is no such thing as one rod length that is suitable for all types of fly fishing. Serious fly fishermen usually own a selection of rods ranging from maybe 6½ feet up to 9 feet. Although fly rods are made in lengths longer and shorter than this, 9½ is about as long a rod as even the most powerful casters can use effectively. This would also certainly be unwieldy for any youngster. A rod shorter than 7 feet, however, does not really allow enough line control for the average caster in actual fishing. I suggest the beginner start with a rod in the middle range at about 8 feet with a progressive bend from butt to tip. At this stage it's best to steer clear of fancy "tip action" or specialized tapers in rods. Later you may want to try these other actions but most experienced anglers use rods with a uniform bending pattern.

Learning to Fly Cast

Fly casting sessions can be started without even leaving the house. Fly casting is strictly a matter of good timing. The beginner stands as good a chance of learning this timing and rhythm as the experienced caster. Actually, I prefer to teach people who have never cast a fly rather than those who have tried to learn by themselves. The rank beginner hasn't got any built-in mistakes which must be unlearned before good casting can be taught.

A relatively new method of teaching fly casting was invented by anglers Lee and Joan Wulff and is marketed by the Garcia Tackle Company. It is called Fly-O and consists of a short rod fitted with a large yarn line. This outfit, along with the accessories, can make the process of learning fly casting a matter of hours rather than weeks or months. The reason it is so effective is that you can actually see the highly colored yarn line unfolding, or failing to unfold, in slow motion. An illustrated booklet shows how the cast should be made and what the sight picture of the unfolding line should be. One big advantage of this kind of outfit is that it can be used for extended periods of time without tiring the casting arm, which tends to destroy casting rhythm when practicing for any length of time. If money is a big item you can make up your own basic casting stick using a three-foot dowel and colored rug yarn. Start by tacking about a five-foot length of rug yarn or ribbon yarn onto the end of the dowel. Cast until you can get a nice tight U-shape bend in the line on the backward and forward sections of the cast. In fly casting all the force is applied when the arm is between the 11 o'clock and 1 o'clock position if the shoulder is considerd as the 12 o'clock position. With such a short length of highly visible yarn it is easy to see where the rod tip (or dowel tip) is at all times. As you become better at casting, tack on longer and longer pieces of yarn, up to a maximum of perhaps 10 or 12 feet. With the Garcia Fly-O you can also practice the other elements of the fly casting.

These practice sessions can take place in most living rooms. When you are able to handle about eight feet or so of line you are ready to try some casting with a regular fly outfit. For a practice fly use a cheap but colorful fly on size No. 10 hooks, making sure to cut the hook barb off the hook. It is best to practice casting on a soft surface, like a lawn. This limits damage to the expensive double taper line.

Leaders and Tippets

A leader is a length of monofilament line that connects the fly to the fly line. Most leaders are made with a very thick monofilament sections near the fly line and thinner line near the fly.

In fly fishing I consider the leader nearly as important as the line being used. Eventually you will want to make up your own leaders but I suggest you purchase a commercial, tapered leader for your first practicing and fishing trips. Most of these

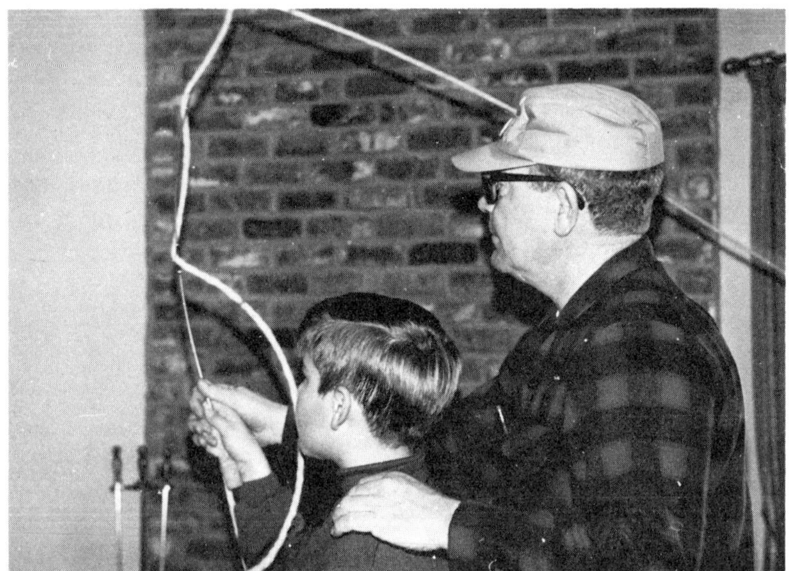

The rudiments of fly casting can be learned indoors, using either a Fly-O or a piece of thick yarn connected to the end of a dowel or clothes hanger wire. Here is the start of the forward power stroke in fly casting.

The line, or yarn, should come straight as possible off the tip of the rod, parallel to the ground. It should form a tight loop.

Beginners have a hard time getting the right timing to make the line, or yarn, shoot out parallel to the ground.

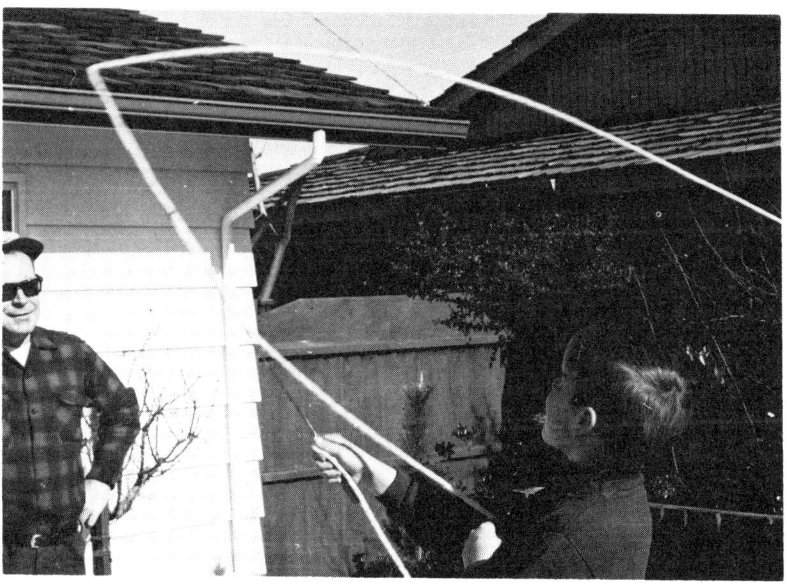

. . . but eventually they master the rhythum needed for fly fishing.

leaders come with a loop at the thick end of the taper. You can tie this directly to the line. Or, you can cut the loop off, make a hole in the end of the fly line (by jamming a very large needle into the end and out through the side of the tough line material about a half inch up the line), and then thread the thick butt material of the leader into this hole in the hollow core of the line, securing the leader material by tying it around the fly line. Many fly lines come with a small metal spear attaching device.

I have generally found it is best to cut about 18 inches off the end of a double taper line before attaching the leader. For some reason nearly all line manufacturers leave about two feet of level line at the end of their lines that works to destroy even the best casts. If you have a selection in the purchase of commercial leaders choose the one that has the largest diameter in the butt section. Even the best commercial leaders are not thick enough to match the tip of the fly lines, which they should nearly do for best casting.

The basic leaders currently sold on the market usually come in either 7½-foot or 9 foot lengths. To start, try the 7½-foot leaders. This size is much easier for the beginner to handle than the 9 foot models. The shorter leader is suitable for fishing the majority of situations.

I consider the basic leader to be a different thing from the "tippet," (the section of line tied onto the leader at the small end). No matter how expert a fly fisherman becomes, he or she casts at least a little bit differently than any other fly fisherman. This doesn't matter except for the extreme effect on the way the fly is delivered at the end of the cast. This delivery can be completely controlled by the length of the section of monofilament used for the tippet.

The ideal in fly fishing is for the fly to arrive on the water with an absolute minimum of fuss and commotion. If the fly arrives with a splat it will frighten most fish. If the energy of the cast is not completely gone before the fly arrives the tippet will fall on the water in a jumble of coils that will discourage even a hungry fish. Also, each size and shape of fly has a different weight and a different amount of resistance to the wind. This is the case even with two flies of the same pattern if both have different amounts of material on them. In any case you can correct this problem with the tippet length.

Generally I will start a casting or fishing session with a tippet of about four feet. On a 7½ or 9 foot leader this is almost always too long. I use tippets made of four pound test material if I am fishing for trout or panfish. I always make a few practice casts. If the fly turns over and splats against the ground I know the tippet is too short. If it fails to turn over completely it is too long. You have to experiment with each size fly until you get exactly the right length so the fly turns over and lands with delicacy. The same applies to the larger, more bulky lures used for black bass fishing, except that for black bass you will be using a tippet of much larger size.

In delivering a fly on the water the leader must be straight once the fly is on the water in most situations. Unfortunately, the leader will usually take a set between casting sessions or fishing trips because it is wrapped around the spool of the reel. In order to get rid of these coils pull the monofilament leader gently with a piece of rubber folded over the line. For my own fly fishing I use a tire (or wader) patch, then if I get a hole in the wader I've got the patch to cover it.

Flies

The number of flies that have been designed to fool trout and panfish and the amount of literature that has been devoted to this subject are almost limitless. Most serious fly fishermen usually end up learning how to tie their own flies because to have a representative collection of even a few hundred flies would cost a very great deal of money. However, there are only five different *types* of flies: dry, wet or sinking, streamers, bucktails and nymphs. Dry flies are meant to float on the surface and imitate some type of land or water insect that is emerging from the water in a hatch or a land insect that has fallen on the water. Wet or sinking flies are intended to imitate insects in the water. Streamers and bucktail flies are meant to imitate minnows or small fish. Nymph flies attempt to imitate the immature version of aquatic insects before they begin to change into adults.

You and your youngster will be confronted with a huge selection of flies when you go to that section of a sporting goods shop. All of this seemingly endless selection of flies can be put to good use at one time or another in actual fishing. But you don't have to wreck the family budget to start a good and logical fly collection. A half-dozen different flies from each different type of fly will be enough to get started. If money is a real problem start out with only one fly from each group rather than a lot of one type.

DRY	WET
Adams	Leadwing
Royal Coachman	Black Gnat
Bivisible	Wooly Worm
Wulff	McGinty
Deer hair	Gray Hackle
	Hendrickson

It's best to start a collection with Bivisible in the dry flies and Wooly Worm in the wet selection. Buy as many of these as you can afford including as many different sizes as possible, even if you can only purchase a single pattern in each size. Size is more important than color. It would be possible for an angler to fish for all trout and panfish species without ever owning any flies other than Bivisible and Wooly Worm, although serious fly fishermen would consider this too simplistic.

The Bivisible is a fly tied with the hackle (feathers wrapped around the hook or body of the fly) wrapped the entire length of the body and a light-colored hackle tied around the front of the hook. The Bivisible was named and designed so the darker hackle at the rear of the fly would be attractive to the fish and the angler could still see it well because of the light colored hackle at the front. The Wooly Worm doesn't imitate any aquatic insect but is meant to represent all forms of these insects in general.

When you start a streamer and bucktail collection select a dark pattern and a bright pattern and buy several sizes of each. A good start might be a black Marabou and a Mickey

Finn. The nymph patterns are harder to find but a Caddis Nymph and a Yellow Stonefly would be a good starting point. Again, try to get them in many sizes.

This may seem to be an over-simplified approach to flies and fly selection but it is certainly adequate for beginning anglers. If your family decides to get really serious about fly fishing it would probably pay to look into buying a good fly-tying kit. Fish are not nearly as selective as fishermen when it comes to choosing what kind of fly they want to hit. So the first few flies you tie from a fly-tying set will very probably take fish, even if they don't look like the nicely finished flies you buy in a store. Fly-tying can become a very interesting family hobby in itself and it allows you to extend your enjoyment of the sport of fishing to all months of the year. For a youngster or an adult there's nothing quite like the thrill of taking your first fish on a fly you've made yourself.

Fishing With Flies

Fly fishing in lakes is a contemplative kind of sport. It can be restful and relaxing for an adult to cast quietly over an expanse of water on a sun-bright day. But this simple pleasure of merely casting while enjoying the surroundings can often be dull or boring to an active youngster. I've found that most youngsters do not sustain an interest in the mechanics of fly casting, which can be so attractive to adults. If you are teaching a youngster who is relatively active it is often a good idea to allow the youngster to fish with the more active spinning equipment while you work the area with flies. Fly fishing can be just as fast and furious as any kind of fishing but the situations where fly fishing is the most productive method of taking fish are more limited than those found when using other kinds of equipment. If you should locate a cove or point of land that has a large number of panfish you will probably start taking many of them with the fly outfit. This is the time to trade off the fly rod with the youngster and let him load up the stringer with panfish.

One of the important reasons for learning all methods of fishing is so you can have a large variety of methods to offer fish. In my own fishing I usually have at least a fly rod and a spinning rod rigged up for each person. They are set up in advance and ready for action at all times so that should the conditions change I am ready in seconds to offer fish an alternative. Often when trout fishing you will be trolling or casting in an area with no visible signs of surface activity; then suddenly, the entire section of lake comes alive with fish actively feeding on the surface. At times like this about the only thing a trout will accept is a fly that closely resembles the hatch that is coming off the water. These hatches can often be sensational to watch and more sensational for the fly fisherman to participate in. They can also be very short in duration. If you have to stop and rig up a fly outfit in this kind of situation you often find yourself with a partially rigged rod when the hatch stops as quickly as it began. And that might be the only hatch for the entire trip.

Panfishing With Flies

Probably the easiest and fastest way to start taking fish with flies is to go after one of the panfish species. Nearly every lake, and most streams at lower elevation, will have a panfish population. Early in the morning before the sun falls on the water, or in the evening after the sun has gone off the water, you will find bluegills and other panfish in the shallower areas. A good bet would be to look for them in coves and near any brushy area. At these times of day, if the water surface is calm, you can usually see the swirls of panfish feeding on or near the surface. This is particularly true during the warmer weather months. In cold weather panfish will be in much deeper water and they will be much less likely to take any kind of offering, other than bait.

One of the keys to locating panfish for fly fishing is to find drowned brush or other protective cover. All panfish need this sort of cover for protection from larger fish. On a blistering hot summer day you will find virtually every panfish in a section of lake crowded in under the shade of brush or rocks. If the sun is at an angle fish the shady side of brush or rocky cover. The process of fishing for panfish is simple. It consists of casting to an area where you see them feeding or where you suspect they are holding in some form of cover and then allowing the fly to either rest on the surface or sink slowly down into the water. With a dry fly allow the fly to rest on the surface until all the ripples caused by the cast have subsided. Then twitch the fly gently. This is normally when a panfish will hit, or at least show interest in the fly. In all fly fishing keep the rod pointed directly at the fly and retrieve or give action to the fly by slowly drawing the fly line back toward the rod. If you are retrieving the line with your left hand place the index finger of your right hand over the line, next to the handle, and gently clamp down on the line as you end each draw with the left hand. This gives you complete control of the line at all times. If a fish should hit as you are reaching for another length of line with your left hand you still stand a good chance of hooking it.

One of the primary objectives in fly fishing is to keep the line as straight as possible between the fly and the rod tip. If you make a poor cast that ends up with a lot of slack it isn't necessary to pull the line back in and make another cast. Instead, pull the slack and loops out of the line and fish the cast just as slowly and carefully as you would a good cast. This is particularly necessary when you are fishing on very calm water, since you want to cause as little disturbance as possible. If you try to pick up a dubbed cast from the water by lifting the rod quickly, the line will make a ripping noise as it swishes off the water. This kind of disturbance will alert fish for a great distance and usually cause them to stop any active feeding.

One reason fly fishing is so effective for panfish is that no other method of fishing allows the angler to move an offering so slowly. It is possible to inch a fly through the water at such a slow rate that you can hardly see it move. Yet this slow movement causes the feathers and hairs of a well-tied fly to wriggle enticingly and attract fish. Under normal circumstances you will want to move a fly through the water, or on the water, as slowly as possible for all species of fish. There are a few exceptions to this rule, such as when you see a fish repeatedly approach a fly and then refuse to hit in spite of evident interest. At times like this you might try moving the fly at a different pace until you either take the fish or it refuses to hit entirely. One of the most effective ways I've found of taking trout, and of locating schooling fish like crappie, is to cast the fly out behind a boat, lay the rod down, with the tip over the stern, and the reel handle up. Then troll by rowing at a very sedate pace. This "rowboat" trolling allows you to cover a great deal of water, rather than to merely cast at random in different sections of a lake. In this sort of trolling it is usually necessary to pinch a split shot or two onto the line in order to get the fly down to deeper water, where the trout and schooling fish are holding. Once you locate a school you can usually catch many of them by anchoring and casting to the spot where you took the first fish. Because fly fishing is such a pleasant way to take fish I often combine two methods of fishing. I use spinning equipment to troll until I locate a concentration of fish then stop and do the actual fishing with the fly outfit.

Flies In Streams

Fly fishing in streams is one of the most demanding forms of the sport of fishing. The two main problems faced by any stream fisherman when fly fishing are (1) dealing with the forces of the stream current and (2) finding areas where the stream bank is free enough of obstructions to make a back cast. These problems are too much for some youngsters; others, however, can become amazingly adept in handling their fly fishing equipment and are fast to learn the ways to deal with conflicting currents.

One way fly fishermen deal with currents is by wading the shallower sections of a stream. Naturally, very small children cannot be expected to don waders or hip boots and enter the stream but older youngsters who can swim and who are careful by nature could possibly be fitted with wading equipment.

The reason wading is helpful in stream fishing with fly fishing equipment is that there is normally a section directly

The kit used by the author to make fly leaders. The leader "book" at the top right stores leaders; the micrometer is used to check the size of lines that are not marked; the tire patch to straighten the leader.

above the stream that is free of brush and trees. In addition, by casting directly up or downstream, the caster who is out in the water has solved the problem of dealing with currents that affect the line by dragging against it between the rod and the fly. A cast can be made up or down stream and the line drawn back through the guides at a pace that matches the downstream drift of the fly, or the fly can be worked upstream against the current so that it is given additional lifelike movement. Even when casting from the bank the fly fisherman will want to make most of his casts by quartering either up or downstream so he has a measure of line control. The caster should usually raise his rod tip as high as possible on upstream casts to keep as much line as possible off the water surface. This will cut the effects of counter currents that intervene between the rod tip and the fly to a minimum. Thc ideal technique is to allow only the leader to rest on the water; however, this situation is relatively rare, except for casters who wade into position to make short accurate casts.

As a general rule I usually fish dry flies upstream and wet flies, streamers or bucktails downstream. In my own case I generally wade as deep as possible with the aid of a ski pole I use for a wading staff. My wader boots are fitted with shaped pieces of indoor-outdoor carpet cemented to the soles with contact cement. I usually select sections of stream that feature rough pocket water because this is the most difficult part of the stream for other anglers to fish if they do not use deep wading equipment. My own method is to wade until I am in perfect position to deliver the fly with a minimum amount of line and leader on the water surface to quiet pockets behind obstructions or interesting side currents. Very probably you will not want to try this form of fly fishing with a youngster in tow until you are very sure that he or she is capable of handling wading equipment. But if you are to eventually become an accomplished fly fishermen you will have to seriously consider buying and using good wading equipment.

Dealing With Line Drag

Even if you decide not to try wading you can still fish many parts of the stream effectively from the bank and from rocks you can stand on along the shoreline. The problem of working a section of stream is the same for the fly fisherman as it is for the spinning equipment fisherman. You should cover the close-in water before you lengthen line and cover areas further out.

When you make your first few casts in a stream you will be able to see the drastic effects intervening currents have on almost every cast. In some cases it will even seem that the currents between you and the fly are actually curling back and going upstream. In fly fishing from shore it is the control of this element of drag which becomes your primary concern. This is more pronounced in dry-fly fishing than when fishing wet flies, streamers or bucktails but it is present in all cases.

You can diminish some of the effects of unwanted drag against the fly by "mending" the cast. Mending a cast means simply that when drag begins to affect the line between the rod tip and the fly visibly, the angler flips a section of the line back upstream without pulling the fly off the water, or while pulling it as short a distance as possible. Sometimes you can mend a cast several times in a single drift and get an appreciable amount of additional drag-free drift. Mending a cast is relatively simple because you can see the line and the effects of the upstream flip as soon as it is made.

Sometimes you can effectively cover the water directly across a stream with a dry fly by quartering slightly upstream when casting and allowing some slack line, coiled in the left hand, to feed out as the current drifts the fly downstream. As the extra line pulls from the left hand it has the effect of eliminating some of the drag that would be caused on the fly if no additional line were applied to the drift. With a good straight cast you can often get as much as 15 feet of drag-free drift with a dry fly.

Probably the two most-used casts for shorebound fly fishermen are those quartering sharply upstream for the dry fly cast and those made directly across the stream or slightly upstream for sinking flies. In the sharp upstream quarter cast the objective is to reach out to pockets and currents on your side of the stream and to keep the line and leader as straight and as drag-free as possible while the dry fly drifts back toward the rod tip. On the sinking fly cast across or quartering the stream you have little control of the fly except for whatever action you supply with your left hand. I usually pulse the fly by pulling with my left hand as the fly drifts down and around in the downstream arc. I often also hold additional line in my left hand so I can let it go as the line draws tight at the bottom of the drift. You will get some strikes when the fly is curving downstream but most hits will occur either at the bottom of the drift or soon after you begin to make the retrieve back upstream. The reason for this is that at this point the fly is deep as it is going to get in that drift.

Depth Control

The depth at which a sinking fly is worked is important. As a general rule the deeper you can get in the stream, as close to the bottom as possible without hanging up, the more fish you are going to attract. For this reason anglers who tie their own flies often add weight to their flies before they tie on the material that forms the fly. These are called "weighted" flies. In most areas weighted flies are hard to find. Usually, unless you tie your own flies, you cannot find them. There are two additional ways you can give added weight to flies. One is to wrap strips of lead, called "fuse lead" wire, to the body of the fly. This fuse lead wire comes in lengths that can be wrapped directly around the body of the fly. The second method is to add a split shot to the line above the fly. Most anglers add split shot some distance up the line from the fly. This gives a very unpleasant pendulum effect to the cast that I do not like. I generally add the split shot by clamping it to the line right at the fly. This concentrates the weight in a single spot and I haven't found that it distracts fish from hitting the fly. In any case, addition of weight to the fly or fly line should be kept to a minimum if at all possible. Each fly line and leader will support only so much weight. Unless the angler is very careful he will reach a point where an overly-weighted fly causes the leader to sag down so much that he hooks himself.

Safety With Flies

The preceeding horrible example brings up the item of safety when instructing a youngster in fly fishing. Naturally, safety should be the first consideration for adults and children alike in all fishing situations, but aditional caution is required when it comes to fly fishing. Hooking most parts of your body, such as an ear, with a fly can be painful but not critical. But there is always the danger of hooking an eye. For this reason I always wear protective glasses in my own fishing and supply glasses to youngsters who do not have them. Dark glasses are rakish enough to be attractive to youngsters and they go a long way toward protecting eyes from the fly. They can also perform another function. Dark glasses with polarized lenses allow you to see down into the water at least 10 percent better by eliminating glare. Since I wear corrective

Surface lures used by fly fishermen to take black bass and panfish. They are designed to imitate land or water insects.

glasses all the time, I use a pair of clip-on polarized lenses over my regular eye glasses when fishing just to get the benefit of this additional water-penetrating effect. But polarized or not, glasses should be worn whenever casting with flies that have the hook intact. Another argument for wearing dark glasses when fishing is that sun sparkling off the surface of water can have a long range effect on eyesight. Doctors agree dark glasses reduce this effect to a minimum.

SPIN CASTING EQUIPMENT

Spin casting equipment is a standard type of fishing gear that much resembles open face equipment. One situation where this type of equipment is desirable is night fishing. The reason is that all the spinning action takes place inside a cupped hood that surrounds the face of the reel and no manipulation of the line is required in order to cast. The primary drawback to spin, or closed-spool, casting is that the friction caused by the line spinning within the cupped face of the reel hood cuts down the distance you can cast slightly. A further limitation to spin casting is that very light lines tend to foul within the housing. Most reels can handle lines of only a certain range. The bulk of the freshwater reels handle lines ranging from six to 15 pound test and are normally fitted only with monofilament. If you stay within the recommended size limits these reels are relatively trouble-free.

A standard spinning reel.

Spin Casting Reel Types

There are two different kinds of spin cast reels. One is designed to be used on a regular spinning rod. It is mounted on the bottom, like a regular open-face reel. The other and, far more popular reel model, is designed to be mounted on the top of a bait-casting rod that has an offset reel seat. In order to properly use this type of reel the angler has to "palm" the reel with his left hand and reel with his right. I consider this a drawback to this type of reel (as well as to bait-casting reels) because in order to retrieve or reel in the line you have to change hands. During a day long session of plug casting it is very possible that you might be just in the process of changing hands when a fish hits your offering. However, I would not recommend against buying a reel of this type just because of this item.

With reels that mount on the bottom of the rod you often have to pinch the line against the rod in order to free the pin that acts as a pickup. The pin that releases the line is released either by backing off on the handle a half turn or by pressing a release button. If you don't pinch the line it merely uncoils and drops the plug or bait to the water. With the other type that mounts on the top of a bait-casting rod you usually release the line by pressing a button with your thumb. In either case the casting mechanics are about the same as for spinning equipment. In order to change to a different size line you have to remove the line on the reel. In some models the drag is preset and you have to use a coin or a screw driver to adjust to a different setting. Other models have adjustable drag features. Despite the drawbacks to spin casting equipment it will come into its own if you do much fishing in the dark. Properly fitted with the correct line it is about as trouble-free as a reel can be.

BAITCASTING EQUIPMENT

If you are going to do very much fishing for black bass you will want to consider the merits of baitcasting equipment. Or if you are going to fish very much in salt water you will want to buy revolving-spool equipment. Both are quite specialized, however, and should probably be the last type of equipment purchased.

The very name "baitcasting" is misleading. Originally this type of reel was designed to allow anglers to use live minnows. At the time about the only equipment available was either cane poles or fly fishing equipment. The revolving spool did allow anglers to lob out live minnows or other bait further than they could with a cane pole. (Fly fishing equipment couldn't cast a bait even as far as a fixed pole.) But anglers soon began using shaped plugs in place of the live minnow and that's what is used today in most cases. In today's freshwater baitcasting outfits a plug of around a half-ounce is the standard size generally used.

When the spool revolves in this kind of fishing you must develop a very sensitive thumb to properly "feather" the reel. Otherwise it will overrun the spool and cause a "backlash". This ability to stop the spool at exactly the right place is usually beyond the capability of most youngsters. And, even though all the really good revolving spool reels come equipped with adjustable spool control attachments, there is always a need to apply exactly the right amount of pressure at the end of a cast.

Anglers with a lot of experience say baitcasting equipment is the most accurate kind of equipment for casting accuracy. This may be the case, but it is also a fact that it takes a great deal of time and practice before you can become proficient in this form of casting. It could just be that those anglers who have graduated to baitcasting have taken more time to learn their sport and are more accurate in their casting as a result.

Matching Baitcasting Tackle

There is as much variety among baitcasting and saltwater revolving spool rigs as there is among spinning gear. But, where you have a great deal of latitude in selecting spinning rig components, you have virtually none when matching-up a baitcasting outfit. To show the degree of specialization, here are the various categories (in which there are many subcategories) offered by just one large tackle company (Garcia): Bait casting, Trolling, Boat, Popping and Surf. This company alone has reels and rods with various features that make them suitable for many more subdivisions. For instance, there are "Worm Rods" specifically designed for working rubber or plastic worms and leadhead jigs. A rod suitable for handling 10 to 30-pound test lines would be miserable for plug casting during an entire session of fishing, just as a rod that will handle three-eighths to three-quarter ounce plugs is far too limber to handle the heavy work of a worm fishing rod.

Anglers generally turn to baitcasting rigs because they want to be able to utilize lines larger than 20-pound test, the practical upper limit for spinning reels. This would seem to mean the only time you need this heavy gear is if you are

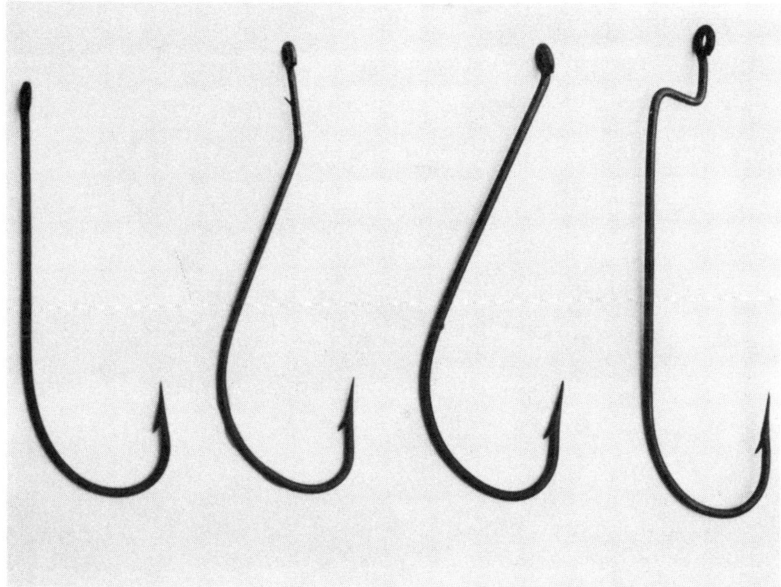

These hooks were specially designed for plastic worm fishing.

going to specialize in this form of fishing. But there is another element concerning baitcasting equipment that needs to be considered in addition to the matter of handling heavy lines. In certain respects baitcasting equipment has many of the elements that make fly fishing enjoyable. It is a challenge to learn how to use this kind of equipment and casting is demanding enough to give more enjoyment than spinning gear to those who manage to become proficient. These elements will probably become increasingly more important as you get into baitcasting. I don't know if you would call this a "snob" value but I do know there are very few experienced anglers who are immune to this sort of effect when they really get to know their way around baitcasting circles.

I'll confine myself here to outlining a basic freshwater outfit that will get most of the chores of baitcasting done. There are so many specialized rod and reel combinations it would be impossible to outline them all.

I think most beginners at baitcasting should limit themselves to equipment made by the few very large tackle com-

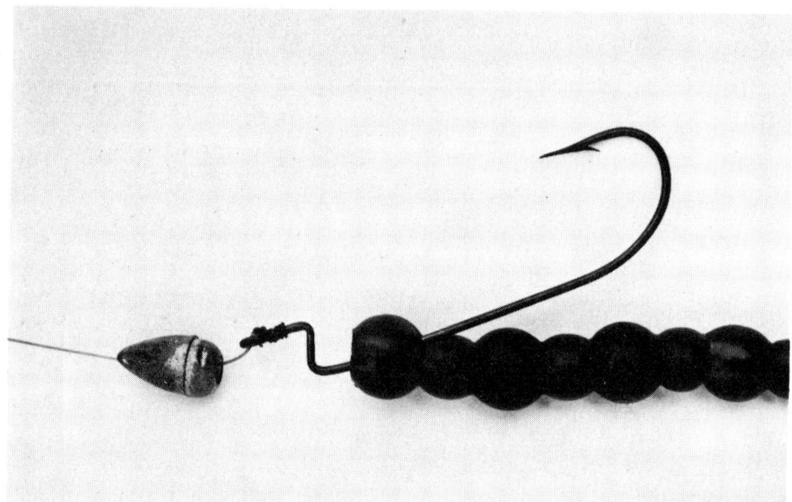

To thread the worm on the hook insert the point of the hook in the center of the worm head at about a 30-degree angle and force it through the plastic.

The completed slide sinker worm rig looks like this.

panies, such as Garcia, Shakespear, or Pflueger. The reason for this is that all of these companies not only produce very fine baitcasting reels and perfectly matched rods but they also furnish lists for the selection of matched components.

Baitcasting Reels

When you chose a baitfishing outfit you simply must be willing to shell out a fairly large amount of money for the reel. A modern, level-winding baitcasting reel fitted with the proper spool adjustment and anti-backlash equipment needed for really trouble-free casts is a miracle of technology and it costs money to produce. In my opinion, a cheap level-wind or revolving-spool reel is simply a complete waste of money from a fishing standpoint. So plan to spend $30 to $50 or even more on your baitcasting reel. Luckily, the rods are not at all that expensive.

The Reel to Buy

The reel you buy for baitcasting should be at least the equal of the Ambassadeur 5000 or 6000 series, the Shakespear Super Sport or Hydro-Film, or the Pflueger Supreme in quality. Personally I use a matched pair of Ambassadours and then match them to various rods in my own collection for different kinds of fishing. Since the rods are not too expensive, a serious angler will eventually want to own several of them. Any of these reels will handle lines from about 10 to 30-pound test. In my own fishing I generally fit these reels with monofilament lines when I am using lines that test 20 pounds breaking strength or less. When you need lines heavier than 20-pound test it is usually best to change over to braided lines, which are smaller in diameter. The modern braided lines of high quality are a vast improvement over lines produced in the past. Some anglers even prefer to use them for all their level wind casting because they have a distinctive "feel" under the thumb that monofilament does not have. Some anglers like these braided lines because they tend to collect a fine film of water that has a cohesive effect and acts as a slight additional brake to retard the spool and prevent backlashes. Even when braided line does get backlashed, it is much easier to get untangled than monofilament lines. In fact, when you get a really serious backlash with the smaller diameter monofilament lines about all you can really do is cut the coils with scissors.

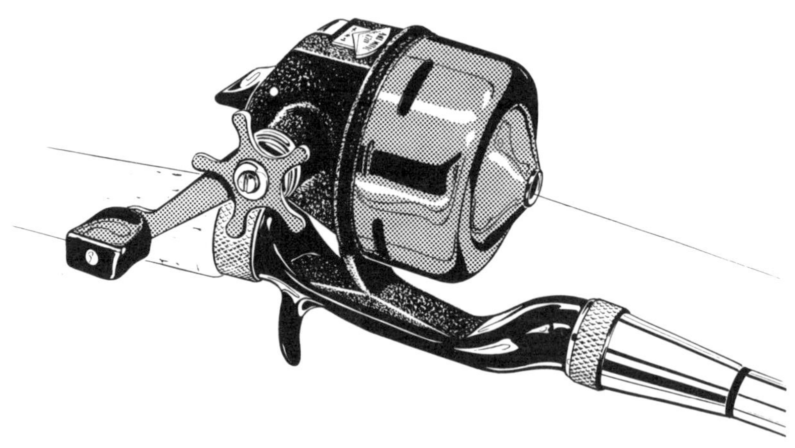

Enclosed spool, or spin casting rig. Note the adjustable drag on this model (star drag on reel handle.)

A variation of the spincasting reel that mounts on the bottom of the rod, much like spinning equipment.

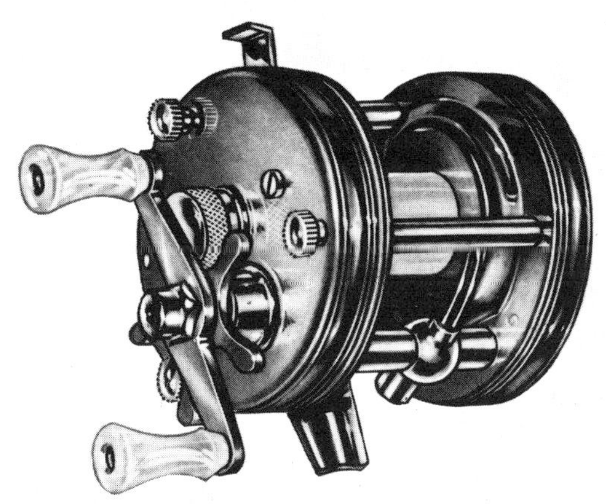

An expensive level wind, or revolving spool reel with many fine features.

A smaller version of the standard-size spinning reel, called Ultra-light; used for delicate casting with very light lines.

The standard-size freshwater (and very light saltwater) spinning reel. This is the best all-round size to choose for the first outfit.

The Rod

When you select your first baitcasting rod you should try to decide approximately what kind of fishing you will be doing. For instance, if you think you will be doing mostly worm fishing you should choose a rod shorter and a bit stouter than the rod you would use for plug casting. In either case the rod should range from five to six feet in length. This is a comfortable size for both bank and boat use. I have several rods 5½ feet long that can be used for the various forms of baitcasting. The major difference between them is how they are tapered. Stiff rods are used for fishing heavy lines; limber ones are for plug casting. Actually, you don't have to be really critical in rod selection. It becomes a matter of personal preference for each angler. A rod that is heavy or stiff to one angler may not seem so to another.

When you make your choice of baitcasting rods try to find a tackle store with a large selection of different rods. About the only way you can make an informed choice between different rods is to have many of them at hand at the same time. It is merely a matter of making your own decision as to what constitutes a stiff or limber rod. If I were to say choose a light, medium or heavy rod action it would mean almost nothing to any other person.

To sum up: as a general guide, if you will be doing heavy fishing, such as that associated with worm fishing, choose the stiffest rod available. If you want more latitude from your rod choose one that is neither the stiffest nor the softest. And, for the very lightest casting choose one with a very soft feel. In this latter category you would be choosing a rod that would be able to do the same work as a spinning rig, and probably the spinning rig would do a better all around job than any light baitcasting outfit.

Using Baitcasting Equipment

The basic movements for baitcasting are the same as those for spinning except there is a very important interrelationship between the forward cast and the pressure of the thumb against the reel spool. The release of the cast is timed by the pressure exerted against the spool, rather than the point of release controlled by the index finger in spinning. To start, adjust the spool adjustment screw on the side of the reel so it will not allow the spool to revolve wildly. This is done by merely turning the spool adjustment screw to the right. This screw can be tightened so it will not allow the spool to revolve at all. What you want at first is to screw it down so it will not allow the line to overrun at the end of a short cast. After making a few casts back off on the screw so it allows the line to run off the reel at ever increasing speeds. Eventually, as your thumb becomes increasingly able to control the over-run at the end of a cast, you will get to the point where you can make casts with the spool running virtually in free-spool. With some youngsters it will take a great deal of practice before they become adept at stopping the speeding spool at the end of a cast.

For casting practice and most heavy worm fishing sessions I

The proper position for the reel in baitcasting, with the handle at an angle almost 45 degrees in relation to the ground.

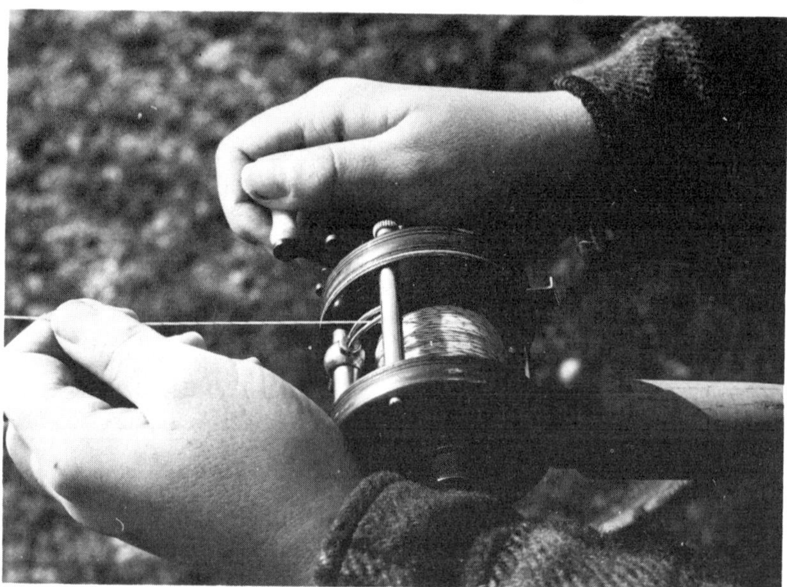

This photo illustrates how the line is fed evenly onto the spool.

Palming the reel when you retrieve. This gives you exact control over the incoming line.

The thumb is used to feather the line. Pressing either against the side of the spool or the surface of the line gives exact control over the fast-moving spool.

advise the use of braided lines of at least 15 and preferably 20-pound test. Lines this size are relatively easy to get untangled if you get a serious backlash and they are strong enough for most worm fishing situations. When using lines of this test you will probably have to use weights of more than half-ounce to get proper casting distance. In fact, for most practicing you should use a weight of approximately an ounce. The first few casts should be lob casts so you can get the feel of the thumb against the reel spool. In proper baitcasting the handle of the reel is supposed to be up and slightly to the right in snap casting. At first, this is an unnatural-feeling position for a beginner to hold the reel in. When you are lobbing a cast this position can almost be ignored. Eventually the reel will automatically fall into the right position when you begin to practice snap casting. When actually fishing with baitcasting equipment, move your lures and baits the same way you do with spinning equipment.

THERE IS SOMETHING ABOUT FISHING

What is fishing all about? For young and old alike, a satisfyingly full creel at the end of a day of fishing is certainly something worth looking forward to. Actually cooking your own catch, after the effort to seeking and finding is a reward far greater than the finest cuisine prepared by a famous chef. There is something about seeking fish and game for the table that touches something deep within the roots of all humans; who were, after all, originally creatures of the fields and streams.

But how do you capture a spring morning when the buds at streamside are bursting with new life? Or the sights and smells of a fishing campfire on a crisp fall evening? It's impossible to put a price tag on the sound of the stream as it burbles across boulders or to describe the majesty of a snow-fed brook rising in the mountain, and to convey the wonder of these pure waters joining with others to form the largest rivers in the mountains. No one can know the greatness of our outdoor heritage better than the fisherman who works the great waters in a valley where the stream has gathered full throat and become a full and complete river. Memories of a crystal day with the water of a lake mirroring a mountain in the backdrop, can last a lifetime, along with the thrill experienced when there is vibrant life at the other end of the line. To most anglers of any age, fishing means much more than just sport.

But fishing is also a sport. Baseball, basketball and football are learned by most youngsters, only to become spectator sports as they grow older.

In contrast, fishing is an endeavor all of us can enjoy from near the cradle to very near the grave. It is a lifelong activity. It should also be an activity that teaches all of the elements of good sportsmanship so often lost in other sports because of the competitive nature. Good manners are as much a part of enjoyable fishing as they should be in all phases of living. In fishing we should always want the other fisherman to succeed at least as much as we want to succeed ourselves. If there is competition on lake, stream or bay it should be friendly competition with a large element of good will. A fisherman deserves the name when he has reached the point where he doesn't measure the success of his trip by the weight on his stringer.

A good fisherman is an observant fisherman. He is just as aware of the croak of a frog in a streamside pond as he is of the action of water on rock that makes a good fish hold. He knows the wonder of the rustle of wind through the streamside brush and the waving grass of the meadow. The cry of a seagull may mean there are gamefish feeding. It also means you have a chance, as a fisherman, to see life in the making, not something that comes out of an electronic box in the living room. The rush of water to a lake or sea shore is as much a part of fishing as the selection of the right tackle for a given situation. There is even a restful element in such mundane things about fishing like the creak of an oarlock as it scratches across the soft air of a summer morning.

Fishing is more a privilege than a birthright. And, like all rights, the sport must be nurtured. In most other countires of the world fishing is the preserve of the wealthy and landed. In the Americas it is the province of the people, all the people. So, it is not enough to merely take from our fishing resources. We should not abuse them. One of the greatest things about fishing is that the angler can have his sport and allow the fish to depart into the water so that perhaps the angler, or another angler, can return at another time to take pleasure with the same sport.

Properly practiced, fishing is a chance to find change from the everyday, the common, the hectic elements in much of today's life. Learning to fish is like the climb to a high place; it takes effort. But fishing is like effortless, exhilerating coast down on the other side. This is what awaits each person, youngster or adult, who becomes involved in the sport and art of fishing.

Index

A
American Fishing Tackle
Association 83, 84
Angling regulations 11
Anti-reverse lever 62
Arc 20, 25, 76, 79, 99

B
Backlash 13, 109, 116
Bail 18, 38, 53
Bait, general 9, 10, 11, 36, 41, 60
Baitcasting 13
Baitcasting Equipment 105
  Basic freshwater outfit 107
  Casting 113
  Categories 106
  Matching Outfit 106
  Reels 109
  Rods 112
    Stiff 112, 113
    Limber 112
  Spool Adjustment 113
  Worm Rods 106
  Weights 116
Basic equipment 7
Bass, black 11, 12, 40, 41, 43, 44, 46, 47, 48, 49, 50, 51, 53, 54, 65, 81, 91, 105
  largemouth 35, 37, 74
  red eye 37
  smallmouth 35, 37, 74
  white 37, 43, 59
  yellow 37
Bluefish 46
Bluegill 11, 12, 35, 37, 39, 40, 41, 94
  local names 36
Bobber 38, 39, 40, 49
  Bobber fishing 10
Bonnet worms 39
Bottom-dwelling fish 47
Bottom fishing 37
Breads 11
Brackish water 43
Brush cover 42, 55
Bullheads 35, 37

C
Cane Pole 8, 105
  fishing 8, 10
Carp 37
Casting 17, 18, 20, 29
  bubble 73, 78
  clinics 29
  closed spool 102
  clubs 29
  practice, use of chairs 29
  practice session 19, 24, 26, 29
  targets 25
Casts
  lob 20, 25, 29, 116
  quartering 67, 99
  short 38
  snap 20, 25, 116
Catalpa worms 39
Catfish 11, 35, 37
Coastal areas 47
Correct age to learn fishing 4
Crappie 35, 42, 43, 59, 96
  Black 37, 42
  White 37, 42
Crawfish 11
Creeks, inflowing 34
Cricketts 11, 38

D
Dipsey sinkers 18
Drift 74, 76, 77
  drag free 99
Dropper strand 39, 73, 78

F
East coast 43
Farm ponds 37
Fenwick Rod Company 16
Fiberglass Rod 16
Fingernail clippers 18, 19
Fish
  Freshwater 35
  Patterns of 55
  Runs of 47
  Stunted 38
Fishing

Fixed Pole 8, 10, 11, 12, 13, 105
Fresh water 10, 11, 16, 30
Guides 32, 33, 47
Months to fish 30
Planning a trip 30
Seasons to fish 32
the edges 68
Fittings 15
Fixed reel spoon 14
Flashers 60, 61
Flies 39, 40, 41, 73, 90, 91
Depth of 99
Practice fly 87
Safety with 100
Tying 93
Types of 91
Bucktail 91, 92, 98
Mickey Finn 92
Dry 91, 92, 95, 98
Nymphs 39, 91
Caddis 92
Yellow stonefly 93
Sinking 91
Streamer 91, 92, 98
Black Marabou 92
Wet 39, 91, 92, 98
Black Gnat 39, 92
Weighted 100
Floats 38, 40
Fly fishing 13, 80, 81
AFTMA Standard 84
Bank Castings 97, 98, 99
Bluegills 94
Crappie 96
Dubbed cast 95
Equipment 82, 105
Matching 83
Ideal technique 97
Lakes 94
Leaders 87, 90, 91
Learning to fly cast 86, 87
Lines 82, 84, 90
Locating panfish 94
Matching the hatch 94
Mechanics of weight 82
Mending the cast 98
Panfish 94, 95
Reels 85, 86
Rods 85, 86
Rowboat trolling 96
Salt water 81
Streams 96
Problems 96
Tippet 90, 91
Trout 96
Waders 98
Wading 96
Food supply 38
Freshwater outfit 17, 107
Reels 102
Fresh water panfish 12, 35
Fuse Lead wire 100

G

Gamefish 11, 35, 40, 41, 43, 46, 54, 65, 68, 85
Game species 38
Garden worms 11, 38
Glamour species 43
Grasshoppers 11, 38
Grubs 10
Golden 39

H

Hatchery truck 36
Hooks 10
long shank 38
Single 49
Weedless 52

K

Knots 18
Clinch 18
Kokanee salmon 61

L

Lake fishing 35, 47, 55, 60
Lakes 12, 34, 37, 40, 42, 43, 54, 59, 94
Leaders 10, 60, 87, 90
Leadhead jigs 42, 51, 52, 54, 99, 106
Level wind
Equipment 13
fishing 80, 81
Reel 13, 109
Line 9, 10, 13, 14, 16, 38, 39

40, 41, 51, 54, 82, 99, 102, 106
braided 109, 113
monofilament 10, 14, 16, 17, 18, 24, 51, 52, 60, 61, 78, 81, 102, 109
snarl 14
twist 14
Live bait 11
Locate landmarks 64
Lures 20, 36, 39, 41, 52, 53, 54, 58, 60
bottom 52
color 59
diving 40, 47, 54
floating 40, 54, 73, 78
high floating 39
poppers 59
retrieve 59
sinking 40, 47, 54
surface 36, 40, 41, 47
undersurface 36
wounded minnow imitation 59

M

Manure worms 38
Maps 34
Marina 42
Meal worms 11, 39
Metal Ferrules 16
Metal fittings 16
Migrating fish 77
Minnows 10, 11, 42, 48, 49, 105
Mitchell 402 16
Moving and casting 43, 48, 49
Muddiness 46
Muskellunge 81

N

Nightcrawlers 11, 38, 49
Night fishing 102

O

Ocean fishing 13, 30
Open face spin fishing reels 14
Outboard motor 47, 48, 53
speed 62
Outdoor columnist 31, 42

P

Panfish 11, 35, 36, 38, 39, 40, 41, 46, 48, 65, 68, 74, 81, 91, 94, 95
Rigging for 38, 49
Schooling 42, 48
Partyboats 32
Perch 11, 35, 37, 42, 43
Pike 81
Plastic bobbers 10
Plastic plugs 17, 18
Plastic pole 9, 10
Plastic worms 50, 52, 54, 106
Plugs 41, 105, 106
Casting 103, 106
Polaroid lenses 100, 101
Popper 41
Practice plug 18
Practice weights 17
Predator fish 42, 49
Prepared bait mixtures 11
Progressive bend 86
Progressive taper rod 16
Protective glasses 100
Purchasing baits 11

R

Red Breast Sunfish 35, 37
Red Ear 35
Red Worms 11, 38
Reel 9, 14, 18, 38, 60, 62, 102, 109
Revolutions 62
Revolving spool 105, 109
Equipment 13
Fishing 80
Roaches 38
Rockbass 35, 37, 42, 43
Rocky areas 43, 55
Rods 14, 18, 41
Bait casting 103, 109, 112
Butt 16
Fly fishing 85
Guides 13, 15, 18

Heavy 60
Rigging 62
Tip 16, 20, 53, 79, 99
Two 62
Rubber worm lures 51, 53, 106

S

Salmon 77
Saltwater
Baits 11
Fish 35, 46
Fishing 10, 11, 16, 34, 81, 105
Migrations 47
Outfit, light 17
Panfish 12
Schooling species 37
Shad 77
Shoreline Areas 42
Sinkers 10
Cone shaped 52
Large 61
Snap Swivel 61
Spawning
Beds 36, 48
Time 36
Spin Casting Equipment 102
Spin fishing 14, 16
Spinning
Equipment 81
Reels 15
Open faced 51
Spool 38
Spinner blades 60
Split shot 10, 38, 39, 48, 49, 96, 100
Spools 13, 14, 17, 18, 41, 51, 52
Sportsmans Groups 35, 47
Steelhead 77
Streams 34, 37, 65
Average size 72
Casting 73
Downstream approach with lures 76
Drift 74, 76, 77
Fast flowing 67
First casts 78
Match the hatch 73
Obstructions 68, 69, 74, 76, 77, 78, 79
Pattern of finding fish 73
Placing bait 65
Pocket falls 69
Read a section of 68
Sizes 67
Sizing up 72
Still fishing 79
Undercut banks 71
Upstream approach with flies 76, 79
Striped bass 12, 46
Sunfish 12, 35, 38, 39, 40, 42
Rigging for 38

T

Tackle expense 13, 14, 16, 17
Terminal rig 38, 79
Thermometer, depth 60
Tidal movements 34
Transportation costs 8
Trolling 59-63
Trout 81, 91, 94, 96
Planting program 36
Rainbow 67
Rising 72, 73

U

Underwater insects 39

V

Vegetation cover 42

W

Waders 98
Wading 96
Water temperature 46, 60
Weights 10, 17, 18, 24, 38, 48, 51, 52, 116
Wobbling spoon 42, 61
Worms 10
Fishing 112, 113
Keeping alive 38